Also by Sotère Torregian

On the Planet without Visa: Selected Poetry and Other Writings, AD 1960-2012, Coffee House Press, Minneapolis, 2012

Envoy, Punch Press, Buffalo, 2010

"I Must Go" (She Said) "Because My Pizza's Cold": Selected Works, 1957-1999, Skanky Possum, Austin, 2002

Always for the First Time, Kolourmeim Press / Co-Published by Pantograph Press, Oakland / Berkeley, 1999

The Young Englishwoman, Privately published by Friends of the Poet, Palo Alto, 1989

Amtrak trek: Being Poems And Prose Written Cross-Country From California To New York, Telephone Books, New York, 1979

The Age of Gold (Poems 1968-1970), Kulchur Foundation, New York, 1976

City of Light, Evanescent edition between San Francisco and Paris, 1973

The Wounded Mattress, Oyez, Berkeley, 1970

The Golden Palomino Bites The Clock, Angel Hair, New York, 1967

Song for Woman, Joycian Court, Newark, 1965

Also from *Rêve à Deux*

Will Alexander *The Brimstone Boat – For Philip Lamantia*, 2012
Schlechter Duvall *The Adventures of Desirée*, 2009

The Age of Gold (Redux)

SOTÈRE TORREGIAN

The Age of Gold
(Redux)

POEMS 1967–1975

WITH TEN ILLUSTRATIONS BY

TIMOTHY R. JOHNSON

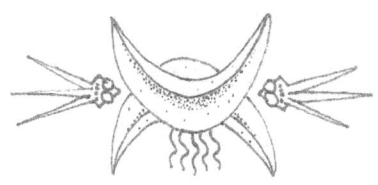

Rêve à Deux

Flagstaff – Stockton – Vacaville

Copyright © 2014 by Sotère Torregian

The cover design is by Thom Burns.

Cover Image, "*Spectre de la rose,*" collage, calligraphy & watercolor, c.1998; page 162: "*Vers Les Printemps,*" collage, 2005; page 184: "*C'est Mon Histoire,*" collage & ink, 2013; page 196: "Footsteps...", collage/photocopy, 2014 © 2014 by Sotère Torregian.

All illustrations appearing on the following pages: Pages i, 2-8, 11, 19, 22, 38, 56, 74, 98, 108, 122, 144, 206 & 211 © 2014 by Timothy Robert Johnson.

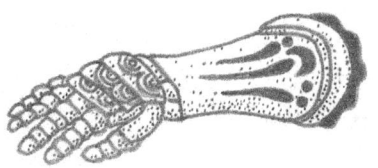

Rêve à Deux

Rêve à Deux was founded in 2009, and is edited by Richard Waara. Additional paperback copies of this book, and other *Rêve à Deux* titles, are available from Amazon or LuLu. All hardback copies are available exclusively from LuLu: http://www.lulu.com

ISBN 978-0-578-13603-5 (paperback); ISBN 978-0-9761436-5-9 (hardback)

Printed in the United States of America

CONTENTS

Drawing: "Beyond Civil Disobedience" by Timothy R. Johnson......... 2
Sotère Torregian: Exquisite Spectral Navigation by Will Alexander......... 11
    Portrait of the Author......... 16

THE AGE OF GOLD

A Note by the Author on The Age of Gold by Sotère Torregian......... 19
    Drawing: "Dream Escarpment" by Timothy R. Johnson......... 22
The Age of Gold......... 23
Is It For This I Live?......... 28
Travois of the Nameless......... 30
Eulogy of the Vain Hours......... 32
For Ted Berrigan......... 33
For Frank O'Hara......... 34
Jerusalem Delivered......... 36
    Drawing: "Cauldron Bridge" by Timothy R. Johnson......... 38
Russian Hill......... 39
Poem Written During Sleep......... 47
Poem for "Half the Population Under Twenty Eight"......... 48
East Meets West......... 50
"Starlight"......... 53
Cecil Taylor at the Fillmore......... 54
    Drawing: "Emissary" by Timothy R. Johnson......... 56
Spectre of Mayakovsky......... 57
For "The Blessed Damozel" of Rosetti, Elizabeth Siddal......... 59
You Warred Against Those Modern Manichean Types......... 60
On the Birthday of Huey P. Newton......... 62

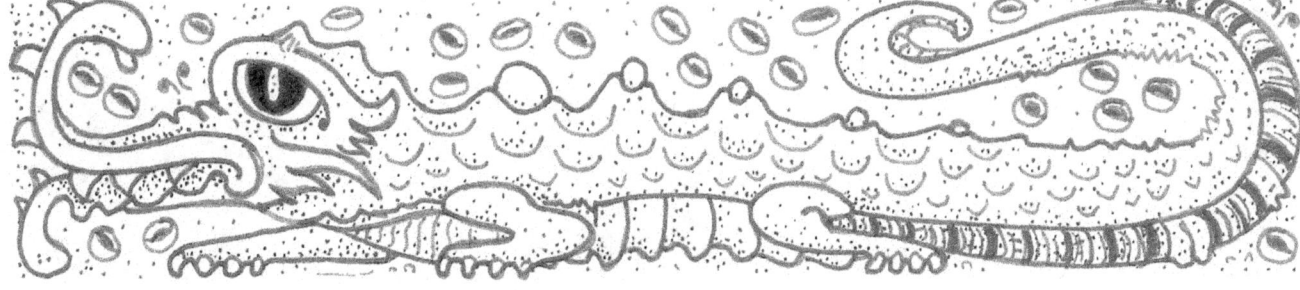

For the Birth of My Daughter Janaina.. 64
At Beethoven's 199th Birthday Party With My Daughter Tatyana........................ 66
The Warsaw Concerto Plays For the First Time on His Birthday......................... 70
For Joe Ceravolo and Mona Da Vinci 71
Spring 1970 72
    Drawing: "The Spur of Chaos" by Timothy R. Johnson.............................. 74
At the Wall of the Sun At the Wall of the Moon.. 75
"Annes" for Anne (Waldman).. 77
Poem for Max Jacob 80
I Am Outrunning the Years 83
The Dutch Catechism.. 84
Jeu de Noël Dream 86
Anya... 88
Poem for Tom & Angelica Clark.. 89
The Rockefeller Building on the Moon.. 90
A House in California !... 91
After the Supremes "T. C. B." TV Special... 92
For Franco Zeffirelli's "Romeo and Juliet"... 94

APOCRYPHAL POEMS
    Drawing: "The Gift" by Timothy R. Johnson... 98
Awakening to the Eroticism of California 99
"The Plough that Broke the Plains"... 101
For Giuseppe Ungaretti 102
Cameo Piece... 104

THE SEX LIFE OF ARSHILE GORKY
    Drawing: "Horse Archers Moon" by Timothy R. Johnson......................... 108

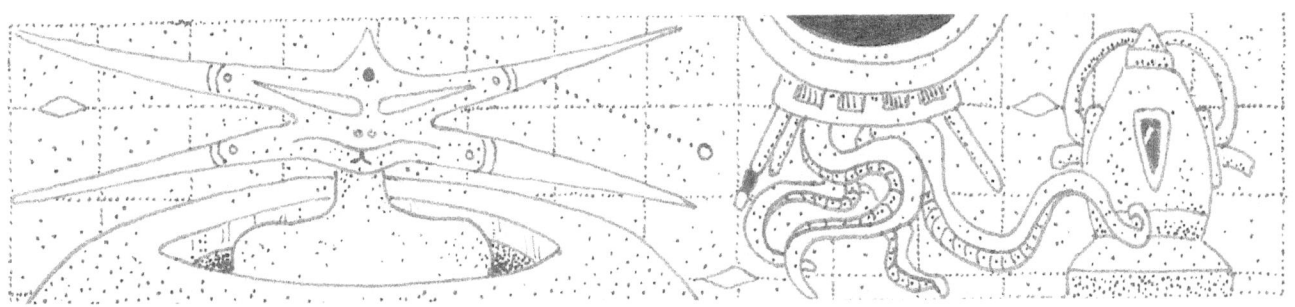

"I Thirst".. 109
The Sex Life of Arshile Gorky.. 110
To Arshile Gorky.. 112
Arshile Gorky – 25 Years After.. 114
"The Unattainable"... 116
"The Liver is the Cock's Comb"... 117
"The Black Monk".. 118
SONG FOR WOMAN
    Drawing: "Enchanté" by Timothy R. Johnson.. 122
Song for Woman... 123
Grand Amoureuse – Anouk Amiée... 133
For an Unknown Princess... 136
Your Name of Gazelles... 137
The "Passionate Affinities".. 140
    Drawing: "The Hermetic Child" by Timothy R. Johnson................................ 144
ON THIS DAY OF CONFLUENCES: The Unpublished Preface........................ 145
REDUX ANNEX
    Drawing: "Diego Rivera's Rocketship" by Janaina Torregian............................ 152
After Mayakovsky... 153
(Farewell to) The Newark Reading Room... 158
I Discover Jean Valjean Everywhere.. 160
    Poéme-objet: "Vers Les Printemps" by Sotére Torregian............................... 162
Rosa Alchemica... 163
The Open Car Door of a Dream... 164
On the Birthday of Pablo Picasso... 165

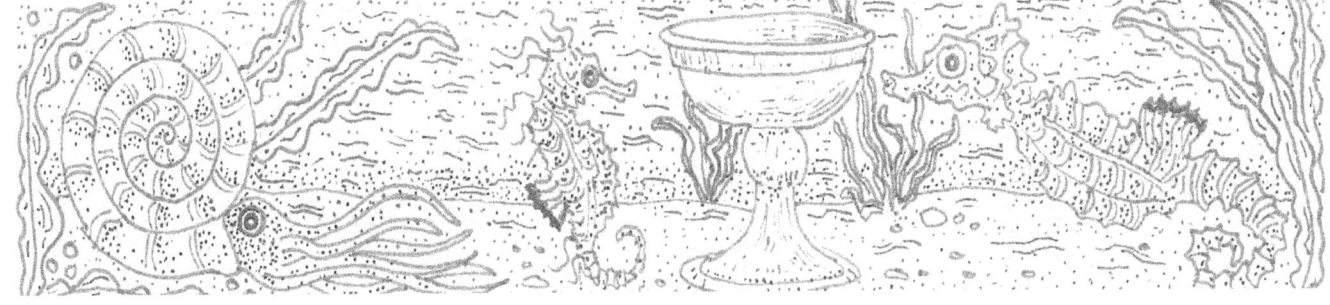

Crossing: San Andreas Fault, April 1968	166
L'Adou, The Woman-Enemy	168
On the Event of the Moon Landing	170
Photograph of the Author by a Santa Clara University Student	172
Forgetfulness (in Arabic)	173
"Night People" in San Francisco on Sunday	174
Point du Sable	176
On Meeting My Friend, Mengistu Lemma, in San Francisco 1970	178
Oedipus Complex, Here I Come	179
"Duck Soup"	180
"Come Back Africa"	182
Collage: "C'est Mon Histoire" by Sotére Torregian	184
Che Guevera	185
For Groucho Marx	188
The Ghost of the City of New York Appears in California	190
The End of the Era of the End	193
Poéme-objet: "Lost steps of the goddess..." by Sotére Torregian	196
The Longest Day of the Year	197
I Did Not Know It Was the Shortest Day of the Year	198
The Mountains of the Moon	200
At San Juan Bautista, A Thousand Years of the Persian Empire on TV	202
In the Poor House of the Wind	204
Drawing: "Spirit of Arshile Gorky" by Timothy R. Johnson	206
ON THE ANNIVERSARY OF THE BIRTH OF SURREALISM	207

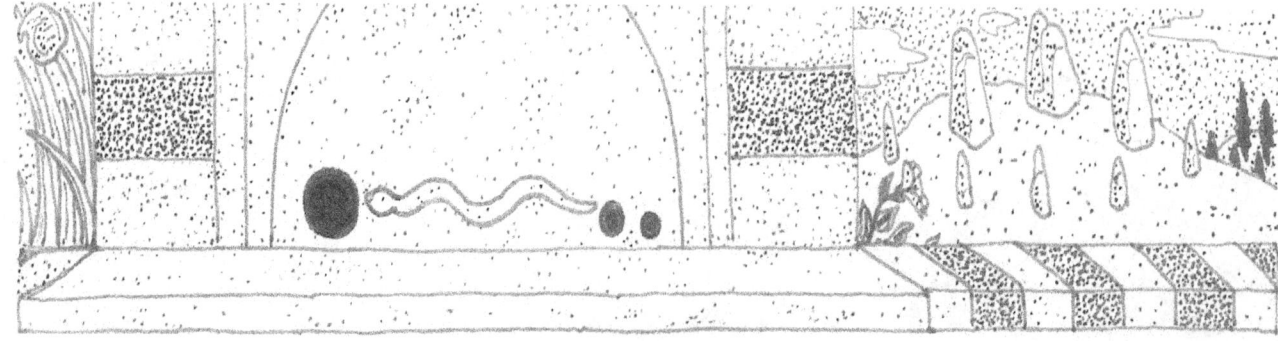

Nota Bene: The Age of Gold (Redux) –
Redux, Reducis, a restoring, returning;
brought back, reunited

— *Latin Dictionary/Latinum Dictionarium,*
Page 292, Compiled by Edwin B. Levine, Ph.D.,
Follett Publishing Co., Chicago, 1967.

Still something not yet told in poesy's voice or print—
   something lacking
(Who knows? *the best yet unexpress'd and lacking.*)

— Walt Whitman, "The Unexpress'd,"
Second Annex to 'Leaves of Grass'
(Italics added by S.T.)

* * * * *

Cercavano il miglio gli uccelli	The birds were looking for millet
ed erano subito di neve;	and were suddenly snow;
cosi le parole.	the same with words.
Un po' di sole, una raggera d'angelo,	A bit of sun, an angel's halo,
e poi la nebbia; e gli alberi,	and then the mist; and trees,
e noi fatti d'aria al mattino.	and ourselves made of the morning's air.

— Salvatore Quasimodo (1901-1968), *Antico Inverno* ("Ancient Winter")
(Translation from the Italian by S.T.)

Sotère Torregian: Exquisite Spectral Navigation

> " A war in the clothes closet is worth a panda on the moon "
>
> Philip Lamantia, *Bed of Sphinxes*

Sotère Torregian's *The Age Of Gold* has come to poetic fruition in a healthless psychic environment, in an American environment subsumed within a degenerative epoch. He has been compelled to survive its tensions by means of a riotous imagination. I'm referring to the treacherous condition which was the New Jersey of his youth, fraught as it was with galling racial schizophrenia. To paraphrase the historian David Brion Davis, racism remains as the DNA of America. At best it persists as a susurrant nettling to all who exist inside its borders. This is a realization registered early on for such an advanced adept as the young Torregian. Given his racial complexification, an ancestry which includes "Ethiopian", "Arabic", "Greek" and "Moorish" amongst others, there is no surprise that Sotère defied and continues to defy assigned racial limit. He could not and cannot be limited to its defined "performative expectations." In this sense he is not unlike Aimé Césaire, his internal identification registers across ethnic and racial lines corresponding to " a path where personal vision, intellectual pursuit, and international movements of art crosses personal boundaries." * Such a vaunted pursuit remains rendered mute within the context of an America that remains imprisoned within the scope of protracted juvenilia. A juvenilia which arrogantly classifies human effort according to winners and losers. From the outstart Sotère was institutionally placed in the loser's classification when his grade school teacher reduced him to the level of "dunce" for not restricting his written expression to "iambic pentameter."

In retrospect such visionless instruction forever stamps its purveyor as a "dunce." And so Torregian has gone the way of Rimbaud by annihilating his early detractor. His language has risen to the level of hermetic seepage, which never opens itself to the profane registration of the distracted reader. It is a hermeticism which obliquely ignites and sets fire to rational expectation. The intervals in Sotère's poems are rife with the unmeasurable. From line to line, from poem to poem we are subsumed by wonders inside maze after maze after maze. Thus the reader succumbs to vertigo so much so that the option of the recreational never enters consideration. One is never reduced to standard fare of, say, reading about the colour of leaves on an autumn day in Maine. We are not subjected to the world of the picturesque, to a facile page of sentiment. Instead innerness persists, a scorched narrative ensues. The reader is singed by vertigo, attempting to pick a lock with a finger of flaming nopal. Which proves quite impossible because his writing is consumed by what I'll call a spectral, a differential physics. When immersed in these works one feels drawn like a phasma across a teeming field of ciphers.

We live in a climate at the cusp of the unspeakable. So for poems to accentuate and tolerate our ongoing extinction remains unabashedly immoral, or to continue to exonerate our general cognitive stasis remains utterly valueless.

Let me say that our species has inhabited for some time this tenuous zone which constitutes the apocalyptic. Within this circumstance regularity can no longer evince itself, so collective habitability on terra luna is now called into question. It seems fraught with abruptness, not unlike the length of a waning December sun. Knowing this to be the background from which Sotère's poetry projects, there can be a no preconceived regalia, no constricted oxygen in the writing. Instead it emits a consciousness which leaves one dazed, much like facing the paradox of dawn on Venus.

It seems as if the spirit of Sotère Torregian has risen from a region of lions. There is no defanged perspective. No inoculation laced with amnesia. His language being threaded with lava and pain, relentlessly seethes with absurdity. Instead of the particular there is the cyclone of the torrential. Nothing seems to escape him. He remains perfectly capable of scribbling on mirrors of scandal. Like Balthus he remains unrestrained by the undertow which continues to etch experience with Victorian decorum. He is not averse to wandering "Under girls' legs" or "...make love with Anne sex..." Instead he crosses out the rules by increasing absurdity. For instance "...A turtle pulls the portrait of a fine lady in white fur toward the smile of a priest" while in the midst of a "... girl who sells fried chicken at night in her cardboard house painted with red bricks..." all the while consulting "... trains of Senufo masks."

Torregian evokes the remote not only in terms of conversational behaviour, but also in terms of its more spectacular manifestation concerning himself with "...the judgement of souls by Anubis/ On the plain of titans..."

When reading Sotère there are times I feel as if attempting to climb declivitous shale. One seems to slip in order to regather footing. There is no place to implement footing, to gather wool about one's psyche so as to contentedly absorb his imagining.

Sotère entrances by the means of an infra-hypnotics which has spiked in his case from the curious power of adversity. I'm speaking of the triplicate affliction of "poverty," "racial" harassment, conjoined with a bountiful "isolation." How else is one spurred to pen in "The Rockefeller Building on the Moon" as Sotère has put it, "I am the exotic animal" who has "forgotten what I was going to say..."? Sotère Torregian remains a living anthem to displacement, to voided orientation, to being an isolate enigma wandering across his own abandonment. One gets the sense of tasting smouldering resin in one's drink.

Torregian has extended Coleridge's conversational profundity into subconscious hoodoo, which "upends dimensions" by he who knows the "science of last things..." Detractors of Surrealist adventure attempt to delimit its navigation to an ersatz capture of oneiric idolatry. This is simply not the case. Sotère proves otherwise. Early on he was entranced by the alchemic solitude of reading. The lingua franca of early home life was Arab and Greek. From the beginning he was exposed to the imago ignota, knowing the strange for the sake of the strange. He was absorbed from youth by an intricate learnedness, which has now developed into a capacious mental stamina. When he speaks of the "...women of Armenia" and makes an intervalic leap making mention of "Maureen O'Hara," he evinces the voracious grasp of his interests. Be it Max Jacob, Vladimir Mayakovsky, Giuseppe Ungaretti, Arshile Gorky, or Che Guevera, we are witness to a blizzard of engagement.

The poems of Sotère Torregian seem at first sight to be a gathering of flawed diamonds which over time condense into susurrant beacons which obliquely blind and transmute the reader at the subtlest of levels.

Let me say that Sotère's poems are not unkempt abbreviations. They work in a register where the initiated dwell, where experience of his brilliance can be shared. Because if there is one thing that can be said about his writing, it is the fact that it remains hostile to facile clarification. It does not court consensus obtuseness. Torregian's work remains far too restive to succumb to the pestilence of capture. This said his poetry exudes an exquisite nobility which has successfully resisted mundane invasion. They exist as spiritual maroons, opaque, threatening, carrying a nameless volatility about them. Sotère brokers no clauses with the author as owner of his texts. He simply receives and emits linguistic ignition.

The editor of this volume, Richard Waara, seems to have telepathically grasped the inner nature of this language, so that it volatilizes each page which is amply sized for its fragments, all the while harmonizing their navigational spectra with the charismatic drawings of Timothy Robert Johnson.

–Will Alexander
February, 2014

* Dale Smith, "Sotère Torregian: The surrealist adventurer of Stockton, California,":

http://poetryfoundation.org/article/238946

The Age of Gold

A Note by the Author on The Age of Gold

> *Grand âge, nous voici !*
> – St.-John Perse, *Chronique*
> ("Grand Age, behold us !")

THE AGE OF GOLD began for me in the state of California.

Having moved away from the hurly-burly of the City, New York, its humid, unbearable summers and bleak winters…

Yet then *The Age of Gold* meant more for me than the locale of a place and its peculiar cultural traits — which were new to me, an inveterate pedestrian urbanite — it was a dream meeting "reality," a quest for the Marvellous across-country, and the prospect of *poésie ininterrompue*, of uninterrupted Poetry.

As its antecedent it was Hesiod the poet/historian of Ancient Greece, who wrote of an Age of Gold in his *Theogony*, the genealogy of the gods, then taken up by Ovid, the Roman, whose epic the *Metamorphoses* prophesied such an age, portrayed as an Earthly Paradise, of *perpetual peace and pleasure*, where war remained unknown and human brother/sisterhood reigned; where fruits of the Earth magically appeared without having to be cultivated; where gods wandered and interacted freely with men and women in a state of primordial innocence.

Thus *The Age of Gold*, as it was revealed to me in these works, opened a new world, a new birth as it were, where all things were possible in a perpetual rediscovery of the Marvellous in everyday life: Beauty of Woman, Dream, Black Humor, and Poetry meeting as one in the *royaume d'enfance* (the realm of childhood) which was an inheritance from French Surrealism, in the poetry and thought of my friend Léopold Sédar Senghor, Francophone-African poet / philosopher, and co-creator of the concept of *Négritude*. *The Age of Gold*, realm of the Marvellous, realm of Poetry itself, freed from the rational mind's confines to become ultimately Surreality.

Yet Thesis and Antithesis: *after* the Age of Gold, as the ancient author predicted, ensues the Age of Iron, to wit the em-battled state of the world as it is in the human panorama of today's newspaper headlines, TV Disasters, wars violence, etc. For me, in the midst of these perturbations, THE AGE OF GOLD continues to unfold.

—Sotère Torregian
June, AD2013

The Age of Gold

Don't talk with food in your mouth
                      During the Age of Gold

We are arrested during your nightmare in Italy

The people rushing by saying we're criminal types
Flush the lantern and beat their belly in a secret language
to Mt. Erynx That's nice I tell one propeller

We meet over the Portinari bridge cross kiss and therefore
      halve it in two greet each other from transposed sides

My hair is not something for like or dislike

A centaur chops off the head of a lapith. Admiral Beatty
      with his *Humph* hands in his pockets wryly watching
      the indigo spectacle

The moon is not red because I have a wife

Lunch is being made in Vischer's King Arthur

Many students of Greek think a thorn of the foot an
    Egyptian bird like a heron
Three tailors of Tooley Street. He was also the chief Moon
    God "wandering the blue rocks"
live with me

Lightning register. All exaggeration of mawkish violinists
Do so with a palm in your throat Pima Indian the Office
    windows from sight

Yet I am just back from three chimeras of world-seeing in
    the Tales from The Vienna Woods

    An immaculate photograph. A signal horse-car
      but took a wagon owing my tongue
As if a Luca della Robbia should be cast in gold shadow
which brings Garbo to a cage of pigeons.
Calling me saluter of the dead. As a funeral of camels
    passes by
The Age of Gold with withering frosted, immodest eyelids.

We do a soft-shoe dance on the snows past. Finally
      standing on upturned
Arrows like the rains of the winds in Holland *softly*.
      Playing hopscotch with
A sphinx. We hear the monotone in Italy. Tropar. The
      fasting ten thousand saints
The transparent dissolving microphone your mouth
      founded for the drowse of Imperial Rome.

Where I am station-caller atop the Imperial Eagle calling
      the headpieces of Maltese Women who bake in the
      afternoon

To them the sea is gauze.

We are arrested
      the *tenebrae* hatchet clicks sparrows

There is a big rectangular hole with mechanical equipment
      within
A bomb settled within & locked up coming out into the
      platitudinous
Sun everyday like clockwork and secreting itself again

            That would destroy the city

        Going through the town of candlelight
We are poor but innocent
The rich section of the town, the unplugged swimming
    pool, are the different foci of the Red Sea

The demolished people are the way ahead

You run away

Where girls are dubbed with race horse wreaths

You return the area is demolished by the robot bomb

Cheese and bread our diet again
We are naked

Is It for This I Live?

    I.

On the street where we used to go to school
We could always tell
when it was going to rain
We could smell the chocolate

It was the factory
of the infinite woman

who would wait for us as a fallacy

As we passed
by the iron grated summer moth
Shrubbery that appeared
on chair coverings in the night they were the atmosphere
by the screened window

II.

A subaltern of desire
Marie, although I don't know why I desired her
    said she saw
you walking in the *tuileries* of the Bronx zoo
inspecting the crushed eye of Babylon

O the *tuileries* will be forever !
and the Bronx Zoo forever
where I will see you walking
playing on the vanquished cabbage-harps of her words

And the observed
connection of any love
we had is
in your hands: a coin bank
in the shape of a lighthouse

Travois of the Nameless
A Memoir N.Y.C.

"Travois," Fr. Canadian, a frame structure by which indigenous peoples, notably
the Plains Indians of North America, hitched their possessions to a horse
in order to transport family and belongings across the plains.

Six o'clock   our passageway tolls in fine pains of The Third World !
On my way home I pass by the bank exhibiting
its trophies   overlaid silver Iago smile
Of "Progress" pulling a diseased rabbit from out of its
Proud and unmoved windows ! Exposing
the African mother with mammalian breasts
O the world without its rest
Travois of the Nameless with their miseries !

An eight-foot sandwichman hands out his last flyer
To me ghost city in the fog
Where I stand Poesy hands out a suicide note to 5th Avenue's
Candy shop & its drooling passersby my map of words
Clientele of ladies in blue sable who come
Into focus one by one out of the throng

Ah Third World my lone epithelium can reach no further
    than the frontiers of my nose !

          From the gorge of the Penumbra
Forever I approach you
        The world without its rest in my eyes
Sybarite who reclaims its immemorial disguise
      Through drawn blinds
Of your rainbow house of wines and spirits !

Eulogy of the Vain Hours
—Matisse

Like hatred when a child falls
That Dreamer again mother Mr. Big
I might be as insignificant as that
In the earthquake of Japanese suns
In the Astrea season false fertile spring of college-girls
All the roads I do not know are painted green
    today
Which means possibly the mountains will die in winter
Which means the people of the earth will wear
Hollyhocks around their ears
My head is a falling comet !
Ah Onto the desert of their tongues
Forty days and forty nights of artichokes
Parachuted poised in my groins their whole upland !

Slowly the caravans take the cellar of the wonder-worker
    away

You are beautiful because I lap under your foot

For Ted Berrigan

Everyone who is anyone is moving away
To — I don't know where
A cow has hung itself in my heart
    because I insulted it with words
I meet the same peripatetic sailor everywhere
    retracing his own steps on aces
    of spades
Holding his speed instrument in his hand.

The "ICE" sign blinks on and off in the night
It is a hungry world
As if I am holding a sail !
Ah Raymond Roussel who invited
    the attentions of little girls !

N.B. : In Mem., Ted Berrigan (1934-1983)

For Frank O'Hara

July 25, 1966

It is in these stones that the claviers sing
trans-quiescent windows We have little money now
All the same direction A pair of shoes found
on our porch   Which can never be known for certain,   for
    no sign

oh monks ! death in an amazed universe
that I can never be tanned enough for
A hysterical girl eating popcorn eyeing Elsewhere
    everyone

"You know, Ernie, this is such a good day,—It's Thursday
    sphinxes
parmigiana cherries limes"
I expect to see you everywhere
In the library of a Big City all the "works" of John Cage

are gone. The anemia of those seeking immortality   After
    you look at her

                              The defoliated
The bowing and "I am guilty" head of a girl as she goes by
Someday if ever I know of a tailor
raincoats   The aficionado   How many *mutations*

of the revolving door ? Camera obscura Always in search
     of those
flaming girls and falangist motorcyclists
The persistence of MEAT LOAF signs
What we can see

The impudence of the struggle !
the tawny enjamb !
Creaseless. Obsidian.
Do not lag withering before Exclude us The washing

Malherbes. Speri. Griefs. Annunciation.

Jerusalem Delivered
for Kathleen Brummal-Torregian

You were admitted to the hospital
and I thought I saw boats float on land
Gangsters played with the sun's paleolithic bones in store front
    windows. Another store window displayed
Apollo Belvedere's genitals
    blackened
A new cult is being formed
as I go by. I hear
tambourines from cellar windows
    A procession for Adonis' death by the boar in the forest of
Our Lady's candles.

My woman the whole earth is being admitted to the hospital
on a rose boat
O hear the singing of the tribe's ecstatic mothers !
In spring clean-up time
They jabbed your cyst like they did Christ's side
    blood flowed
I threw a grenade at medieval times
that allowed women to be burned as evil

See the German girls standing there in the damp night
in front of the *Hotel German-American*
looking for a Third World cock to suck !
I pass   Pass Fantomas to their blonde hair umbrella for my shadow
Oh he is not dark enough ! they say

You bet your life I say into the night
I rescue you a Saracen girl
I throw a grenade at "Jerusalem"
exploding camomile lotion, which does not "form in your hand"
I fight you like an Indian of the Wild West
      a knife fight in a river you win & wear my red shirt
"Jerusalem" is delivered
thousands of cysts happen every year
part of the earth is ugly part of the earth is beautiful

Russian Hill

for Tom and Angelica Clark

A man like snow in Paris beautiful machine
Riding into the stars
A world of "Michaels"
You can blow it like glass I have never seen

The rip-roaring songs of the ladies
Make gold coins
There is a form of a dead horse
In the snow of Indiana
The sun is going down
The sun is going down

Hunter Helen Da Vita Tribute ! Ignite
In Her Honor the contents of four
Medium sized ashcans. Throw in nickels as many
As possible into the flames
                all the while

I greeted you like a long lost palm tree
Palm tree you were and *are* my labor

The Home of the Ten Most Wanted Men
Skillets us. I can find no formality

Except for nurses peeking over the clouds
And answering to my malady in the music of "Red Cloud"

       Terrific forces under the
Earth pushed up.
All the force I lifted as the light part
Sank.

Who will write of the mortality
O mortal of the chemical musician ?
Eating a prohibited Danish
The old lady in the bakery saying " I 'll eat
Some of those today "
Policeman of the zephyr ! Queen Mab rod !
Agha Day
  Space For This Machine
Is Donated

At night I search on the mammoth's
Skull
O Sunday donuts of spring !
The feces of little children lies in your lap !

Greetings we can't remember one day from another
In an anonymous desert of food
I always wave my white blanket to
Greetings thousands crowd the great tent
Although I think they are in error
Greetings we can't remember who you are

To be in this strange city of sparks
Where I can roll and roll forever
I have messages of the sword which are
My menial oracles
My wife a pinpoint
Although she is with me nearby forever coming
Forward on my knees of the lamb
Cyclists of the Auberge !   who are really trees !

      "It would be an interesting risk"
The vast telepathy of death hello this is your mommy deposition
O the infernal Milesian punch proffered us sprockets

We never budge, uncontrolled from the top
And we laugh when doubtless
Being "nice" with a comfortable platoon

Hear my flag, dawn
My intravenous architectures
What I haven't even started yet
In going from one place to another

    Conspiracy of huckleberries everywhere.   O jowls
Giggling and kicking at me
That I find a please key
To the tin calendar

        Do not drop your letter by my wayside
Much of what I've carried with me
Santa Clara !
   Adultery of the throat
A lullaby still throbbing handed me
By silver arms which I chop off
In the blindness of the hot afternoons
Coming into a remembered terrain.

After this encouragement
I am putting up my wings in the orchards
They are really kites
With the signet "Man in the Moon" on them.

The minute moon goes up and down at once
Approvingly and disapprovingly
Inside the gigantic fireplace formed in an owl's shape

It is the whole landscape painted orange

"O maiden   Sprung of water !"

In detestation of my travels
   Thunderherd   Maundy
Yami

Cupola
    Watermelon in the air
The birds take flight

The *cri* of Cerkowitz

War of errants and guides
Time of Census-takers
Dragoons Nocturnes Plead my case
That everything would be volatile child-piano again
    That we could recoil
Uphill to us

But you are loving as a sand dune All tresses of the dunes !

We are the first employees
In your Jules Verne country standing legs spread
Wide apart over the *Mare Tranquilium*
A shoe flies out of the window   (*flop!*)
Your mother and father send up a distress signal
Of jewels they retire to bed like Alps.

If at the ulcer where I stand
All lies bleeding in stamps
O laborers
For the afternoon telephone of "...Dad
Can we borrow ?"

The racing car dances
Living room of midnight
I have the plaint
Of Wednesday in the dog.

These, then, are the much more sober lives

O plain and sky coming in wearing
An evening thatched mask of Nairobi
Where my creation is most natural

Of things *seen* and *unseen* I am the wheels
Light that goes everywhere !
So that in the light still I see
There isn't any garb
That's too meaningful
That Bethel model airplanes

The ground is familiar
Southern Coast of the woman with concealed gun
And twenty four babies
Grinning the rose
What mortal had heard as we have when
Molten mistakes take flight.

When it has wrung its (seals) white
I have gone to its nipple shore
When I'm sick
O Coptic zero I scrounge

Every time a "Refugio" quick
Policeman lights in the chest
In case turns tumors of bikes into
  Old childhood friends

Hi ! Ballet lessons of the swart,   leave
        your triangle to infect others
And go elsewhere

You take too seriously
I must go about my business

My armband must think
        in the recital snows: Permanent

Ah   Thank you rush heading
In the sleek county offices Tests should be fun

        When you've picked a bald eagle
                clean
We're all afterward
In this space I have left to myself
Where in the hangar in doldrums the
Daughters of aristocrats propel   in aesthetic urine
The confusion
Voyageur
That comes out of here anyway

                February — May, 1967, New York City
                        & San José, Calif.

Poem Written During Sleep

Epure si mouve

    The blonde mouths are awake on the tree
where you sleep.

    I recline and awake from time to time
always near my spiritual accordion
Like a plain.

    I can hear myself calling out orders to myself
on a cactus microphone.

    On which rain collects like dew forming an invisible
windshield.

    A tree is weeping in a gutter island that surrounds
it in a storm
    I rest with my hands on your head like a captain at the
helm.

    My hunger yawns in public events.

    A visible voice sings: "The breakmen of the airplane's
harp are sung to sleep," in beautiful tones.

Poem for "Half the Population Under Twenty Eight"

Now the Missal is outmoded
I fondle its ribbons' music
As I stand under this human porch
Made of all ages and climes.
"If you don't mind a little cork"
I ponder
About my nickels
And everything in motion today's
Happy birthday
"I think heroic deeds were all conceived in
　the open air"
The nearest *exit*　"Airflow"
As always.
The Mechanical Ballet.

　　"Dinner", for the cornucopia
Comes home
On a thousand misplaced
Fathers

In their trance
Of transition
The young girls (daughters)
Formed this porch
It is very pleasant when I remember
Their pee is like snow
Or rain depending on their particular (abstract)
Virginity
I am reminded It is too late
Of that inverted Virgin in the crystal glass
Falling forever
O but this is far more tender
Are they here
My substitutes?

March 17, 1967

East Meets West

for Kathleen

We are so far alone together now

On a plain with a TV who is a marksman
Away from "home"
The Great Ball of Times Square hits the pins of 1968
At the stroke of midnight
    This time to the music of *East Meets West* by Ravi Shankar
You lie awake
Like a filmy-door opening to the fig-juiced version
Of Astrophel & Stella

We talk of the great Megaliths around the world
We are as evanescent as
This
My 148th Poem for the New Year

This has been the Appian Way

of friends

When I turn a small light on in my room
At night darker than a father
All this time

I've just realized it now
A little vain milk all that is left of student Rhenish days

The doors open
Ah Clothes ! smelling like a nunnery
The insides of pockets hanging out
For a moment like loose tongues
How sleek he looks !
How sleek he looks ! across the street
   I stand in the arcades with the men like penitents
fingering the girlie magazines

       O   unmarked annals
the civil engineering of the damned !

* * *

The one you're changing to
I feel you go without even saying goodbye
Yet poetry which doesn't begin with this "modest appointment"
Making a cheese sandwich out of the calendar of
Events
You are sincere

I learned my first words from the movies
                  "The House of Rothschild"
    which starred George Arliss who looked like my grandmother

I thought so then "To live with dignity"
Everything is fugitive and nothing is done

You are on the edge of a great cataclysm
The goddess Diana did not prepare a dinner for you
In the railway station at Maplewood for nothing
Although it caused you pain
You cannot seek for its Byzantine miniature
Until you have made it yourself
Each Valladolid led to another
Until you are finally where you wanted to be   In the dawn
    of the star   of the sea

                                        Palo Alto, California
                                        1968

"Starlight"
for Daniel Berrigan, S.J.

I see Autumn's searchlight veer   and *grrrr*
in the dark cold sky
The smell of pizza down below
triples Hecate from an ancient relief
The steel tear on the face of the woman matador

O in the time when bus drivers will do a little
Soft-shoe dance for you and sing you "Country
& Western" music
And wives shoot arrows out from behind their
windows of sleep
"The Bureaucracies" put the passion that consumes me
from within
       between two slices of agony
and eat it like a sandwich
While I'm left like a polar bear without his underwear
    for the President of San Salvador's petite
                      daughter

Cecil Taylor at the Fillmore, San Francisco

New Year's Eve, 1968
for Maureen and Mike Smith

The clock is ticking out the ages of the Ice Age
And should the girl lean up to kiss it
Thanks to our movie industry
The minute hand moves away entirely OFF the face to say
Nobody should think I'm important
For these plane waves
Like the bomber in the head of Mayakovsky
One cannot fail to see the humor in it
Which is   inevitably
Black

The buffalo stops at the shrill of the police
    whistle
Informing us on the spot that our
Rinkety tink of the stars coffee-stained
  studded dogma
Its obsolete   *oggi me voglio piangere perche*

ma uno frammento

del " Principe Africano" anche io
retrove menze il mio
penzare * the imperfect mellowing of suede
    jackets
When the wild horses come from Central Asia
in my expectation
I don't greet them any longer
in the useless ice-cycles

In the morning ping   ping   ping   drugstore of my life

The footsteps of madmen walk
on the quiet of my words
  They will kill Sirhan
The streets lined with gold are belching

---

*Starting from the previous page, translating the Italian: "Today I want to cry because... my one fragment... the 'African prince'... as it is I find amongst my thoughts..."

Spectre of Mayakovsky

> " *Qu'à me pencher sur le précipice* "
> André Breton *L'Air de l'eau*
>
> ("That has me looking into the precipice")

Dream powder of
Your flogging divine Mayakovsky
Throughout the discothèques monsters of dissonance

I would be drunk for the rest of my life

O Mayakovsky Mayakovsky everywhere you are
Turned to stone
In Prague
In the islands of my forgetfulness
in my sweat
        In those who would build their memory
At the center of the memory bank
Lies your heart with its singular inscription

"Postcard From Coco Palms"

O in the supermarket murders of cross-eyed
    children
Of which I still have the bird's feather
                From its crash-site on my
   chest
O Fare Ye Well Merry Widow *Panem et Circenses*

Bridge with a sharp growl

O Benjamin Bufano   broken guitars

      As I contemplate all those truly great
in the bathtub of my Sister-in-Law Maureen
A dragonfly gets washed down the drain
Along with the Venus of Willendorf piece of soap

For "The Blessed Damozel" of Rossetti, Elizabeth Siddal

Cytise aubour saluez vos dames

(Laburnum greet your women)

You Warred Against Those Modern Manichaean Types

You warred against those modern Manichaean types
You were the machine-gun of the Apocalypse
The cults
Of Onan and Isis in whose night I go open-shirted
In whose night I am a slave
You freed me
In winter of the theater marquees
The high-priest's ear cut off

There is a black cloud
In the electric carts they've brought from the Cushman Bakeries
I have seen the emigrants of 1970
With hardly a smile so well-behaved in knowing the
                                                "new math"
You wouldn't know they were children
Everyone sees the half-moon that is his sister
In the ermine of deceit
Pass by like the milk window of a train   Ah young scholars

Hiding your heads like forests I row among you !
Guillotined by my name

Ah planners, burst your bowels !
Over your categories
Over Abe Lincoln
Over your decemvirate
Over your gym-shorts

To Father Camilo Torres Restrepo, revolutionary priest who resigned from the church, killed in the mountains of Columbia in 1966. The " Camilo Torres" Clinic was commissioned by Fidel Castro in Havana, Cuba, in 1968.

On the Birthday of Huey P. Newton, Written for the Freedom of All Political Prisoners

This birthday card
Comes into your cell
It is a birthday card you cannot see
It is signed by the *nameless*
It is signed by dreams
The endless dreams of man of the Primal Peoples
    By their fires tonight
It is signed by Chaka
It is signed by Atibon Legba
It is signed by the blood of Sharpeville
The skull of Vacaville is coughing
It is signed Always in our embrace by Niccolo Sacco
And Bartolome Vanzetti
It is signed by all the Unknown Soldiers hidden
Under the sidewalks on which we walk
It is signed by our glass hands
It is signed by all the watercolors of the world's children

It is signed
By the birds
And the Dolomites that make music
It is signed by the Apollo Club of Harlem
And the songs that are not ours
And we wish were ours
It is signed by the Dome Of The Rock at
Jerusalem
It is signed in peacock
By Billie Holiday
It is signed in my lost hours
It is signed in hunger gazing at luxury
And the stars that fall from the sky
It is signed by the painters of the Lascaux Caves
It is signed by rivers wearing smiles of snow

It is the Birthday Card of the World

For the Birth of My Daughter Janaina

Janaina Torregian, b. 25 March, 1969

Through Polaroid windows everyone looks black
The girl comes out of the Med Center doors yelling Woo Hoo Woo Hoo !
And makes a fire in the rain
As I wait outside for the kingdom of Cush to pick me up in a car
        O Almoravides !
I'm a blackguard in a tower of centipedes
Do you know my address

The glass eyes of Ireland   make me

    anonymous

"I'VE JUST BEEN DREAMING about you !" says the Tartar girl
"Is *that* why my wife's in labor ?"
"Yes."
Hiccups and she-saucers
The ethics of fathers which would not steal money
From your coat while you're waiting inside

Amazed by the dark

The boom gets you   Lanovacs* drop from my nose

Civilized for my bad manners

In the critical eye this time of my Brothers who are maintenanc'ing

      At that moment ventriloquist dummies

Piled on a gurney are wheeled in

    shrouded like statues in Lent

Subba   symbol of   The Great Life

I hope I am not under any wrong influences at this time

        the testimony long and continuous

You're prettier than W. C. Fields

Which makes me dream of cruelty in hospitals

Remembering the summer when the leaves

Treated me as though I were a "destined" Anglo-poet

Made an atheneum-cradle for me

Now girls kick their lovers in the behind

Sons taller than their fathers pat their fathers on the head

Cacti do a rumba   Into the "Brown Bag" Room

    White buffalo skin, hanging on my idleness,

Am I saved am I back again, too stout ravine?

---

*The author recalls hearing on T.V. as a child, circa the 1954 U.S. Midterm elections, a newly invented word, "lanovac," used in political ads of that day to designate a lazy, non-voting citizen.

At Beethoven's 199th Birthday Party, Union Square, San Francisco, With My Daughter Tatyana

" — *Beethoven, one of the greatest Germans of Negro Ancestry*" — *J. A. Rogers*

The coffee's cold already   give me a big slice
Of cake
I can see King Massinissa popping out of the middle of it now
With a machine-gun but this time it's friendly (made out
        of confection)

The biggest birthday cake in the world
Sounding the white shoes with the clicks on them
Of South Sea girls
The way whiteness is born   and prized by those
With darker skins
I come
With a roof of red letter words on my back a wishbone crowing on top
    I'm helpless
"Music is the purest form   of art"
Beethoven, we are here !   Senegalese tirailleurs
At 12.00 noon Greyhound-bound for UNION SQUARE and your birthday
Party   They're giving away a large Cadillac   Ah

   All this is in your guest book Beethoven
The Brother who looks at the morning paper and sees *Football*
Star Is Suspect In Rapes
All of these are in your guest book Beethoven
     Wax on the Suburban Symphony of Fire
You stride pride of Guinea like a tiger in a sports jacket
Dream of a word which revolves around your health charisma and
         my somnambulist departure
An enormous blemish on the landscape

So here's a toast to you my Brother and the world you must
   contend with in your 199th year
The future belongs to the fit   Drive-In movies,   the land,
     the forests mountains and cemeteries,   the sea,   the Bay
        Of the Pacific
   the Indians,   the Eskimos,   the Bronx Zoo,
  Angel Island,   the Golden Gate.

Today
My African Prince

You share your birthday with the depraved hustlers mountebanks
— & just "plain folks"

                Executives off on their lunch hour and the poor in need
The jazz band on the podium playing off-time Dixieland
While they fix the Christmas lights not at all like New York City

                                                                       Old
Dilapidated members of the Garibaldi Brigade Stonehenge foot-women

                                                       It's all over
The musicians returning "Red Garter" on the back of their red jackets

Everyone trying for that one last piece of cake
By six o'clock it's all gone flayed down like a waterfall deck of cards
While I'm losing my hair and
Cable cars are shaking hands

   Jongleur of Saba !
Beethoven when I thrilled at your music as a child
My eyes did not see with their true color Now they do It's a lone
Swart hand that goes to meet yours in this multitude
And your blood remained a deflated chord
                                            on a box - organ
Which leaped up at once to *embrace*

In its one chance the freedom of man in the *Eroica*
        disillusioned
               and deflated again
            This time
                      Your plaquette like a star
        Melting into itself like a block of ice

And in the choruses of the *Ninth Symphony* the rain
    forests of Africa ensconce themselves
    listening for their own echoes
Saying secrets that had "things" been otherwise
Had your *music* not saved you by entering you
Into the salons of Europe
                instead of laurel
    You'd have been led
                    with a chain round your neck
By the express train of "genetic time"
I laugh with flies in my eyes
With my heart big enough for any little animal

                        December, 1969

The Warsaw Concerto Plays for the First Time On his Birthday

for Joe Ceravolo and Mona Da Vinci

The Warsaw Concerto plays for the first time
In my childhood
The pilot has crash-landed
And the beautiful woman is holding
A chrome-plated gun on him
I'm hiding under my seat
In the movie house
"Twenty-five years pass"
In the venetian blinds of tanks lightning.

Once again the Tartar is drinking his own mare's blood.
He needs either Listerine or a record
He walks right into the door-jamb of Adam's Rib
Half asleep   At the "cue"
A beautiful black model comes out wearing a rabbit coat

    My Desconsorts
I fall in love with your image a hundred times
Your shadow in each face I see
As in a "jumbo animals pack" I am the ringmaster
in an interlude in Budapest
when you look out all
from rainy windows.

                                         June, 1968—1970

For Joe Ceravolo and Mona Da Vinci

I sleep in you Great House that sleeps.

Spring 1970
for Bill Berkson

Just give the elevator operator your name   (*Heh heh*)
and he will open the stairway
for you

Just like all Museum Directors
who've never seen
Monsters who couldn't take the elevator before !
Why, my friends ?

It must be a special night
The romances are all glances
Gone for mail   I slip him my name as always   as
mispronounced   besides   little puppie dogs coming
and going out of his accent   the same as in
every other Spring   Ah
The war of the Midi and the Mini is "on" !

Enacted in my mortification   Spring time of the hangman   bristling
Muzak in my future false teeth doing a rumba with
    the "keys of the kingdom"
with the crater *Mount of Venus*   on the moon   condoms
Stealing the art treasures of Navarre

(*Song*)
 "*I'd love to be in a whooping crane sandwich with you*
 Where all the elevator operators would no doubt belong in a zoo
 I'll give it a try, unscrupulous bastards"
 But you would be an unscrupulous bastard and take it away
 from them
 Like a phoenix sleeping under the ashes
 You hear me calling with my Boo Hooo Hoo — Zut !
 All of our Polo Stars go to "cultural events"
(*End of song*)

  "GOING UP"
A little sidewalk of New York broken off is coming at me now
Leaving my fingerprints in New York
I don't know but my size 12 shoes can't see you very well

I am like Mayakovsky saying *My son my son*
at the other end of a dinosaur telephone
On the elevator
are the arms of my Sister-in-law Maureen eating spaghetti
the arms of my Brother-in-law leading a line of "J.D.'s" on a silver chain
   from Juvenile Hall how lonely
  a bottle of *Liebfraumilch* with wings

At the Wall of the Sun
At the Wall of the Moon

On trips to the local library, Tatyana, my daughter, and I discovered, in a children's book, the UNESCO paintings done by Joan Miró. I owe my passage then through night to my two daughters, Tatyana and Janaina.

To the furies of Nothingness who day and night whistled in my ear
I laughed
At the Wall of the Sun.
The clock lost its combination   Ziegfeld was not dizzy
But exchanged horoscopes. Every night language heard in the house
Lemonade Soda Water Seltzer Tonic Ginger Ale Sarsaparilla
Champagne Cider
An inspiration to the beautiful women made in the image
Of the Avenue that smokes too much and brings me back
Bad memories without even the decency of calling me by my name
I wept
At the Wall of the Moon.
The falls frozen in the guise of an "ice dinosaur ghost"
Began to sing an aria Zing Zing Boom Bay
The Amazons of Songhai astride their mounts armored in quilted coats
Stop on a dime right in front of me   Eros of blonde furniture

In the legs that haunt me everywhere of the mother in a mini
        crossing the street with her baby
Your voice grows younger while you grow older.
When you watch the red clouds at the end of day
At 6 o'clock P. M. little bulls come out of your tears
No matter how many mistresses you might clothe yourself with
Inside, the fire station has its own dissident members who, when they hear
The clang, retire. The red tie remains aloof in its aloneness
Of "Screen Stories." The emerald eyes of dowagers say "O you're my
        hobby.   How interesting !"

To the quivering teeth of swamp-madmen on street corners

"Annes" For Anne (Waldman)

I know so many "Annes" they leave me speechless.
All of them have come from "Anne" heaven
Down to earth at me like a milkshake round my head giving off
A halo. All of them make love with "Anne" sex.
When I was a child I wanted to marry a girl with the name of *Anne*.
All our friends named "Anne" live in Anne houses
And in the blush of Sunday go to little out-of-the-ordinary
Anne churches with "ice-cream cones" on top of them.
They're experts and study Anne languages like Spanish French
And sometimes Russian in this way they have created themselves
"Ex Nihil" out of nothing. All our Anne friends come from Anne
Countries and have Anne complexes about their "unworthiness"
All our Anne friends have an Anne relationship to an
old lover they want to forget. "Anne" is a common name
But all the Annes I know are not at all common
There's Anne of the boot Anne of the whip Anne of
Queen Anne Lace. Anne of Sojourner Truth. New York Annes California Annes
In their Anne rooms cuddle up around a book with the light
"On" at night. All my Anne friends give me Anne sympathy

For my world-weariness.   They write singing Anne letters
Which we receive from far-off places.   Every Anne is aware of
The hypocrisy of "socks" with which I have to struggle every morning
And from which, standing off with guarded amusement, all Annes are
Immune.   The blue of the summer beach is in the name of Anne.   Anne-tan!
I bear my wounds with a solemnity I would think "worthy" of dedication
To the beauty of an Anne. Anne solitude like the refried bricks
Of the tears of Pompeii. Somnambulant Annes. Annes in bathing suits
playing in the snow of New York from which I am a Napoleonic bear
In exile forever. Annes laughing when I am standing around in my
Undershorts late for work. Annes saying their one and only
Inimitable Anne "Hello" to a baby. My reverence

                                                                                               hovers over

The pristine beauty of Annes when they wake up like a Spanish
Galleon trying to dismiss the night before.
The Annes admiring Indian miniatures and letting their hair fall
On them as they look. Each Anne that I meet by chance
That I shall never meet again. The "Anne" standby or Anne proxy
Always done in good humor at baptisms or other major events.

The praises of Anne in the Ethiopic Liturgy at sunrise.
I am surrounded with Annes a map of the Annes of all the world
Naming the Annes I know that come through me with or without me
The hands of the invisible Annes that massage my headaches
The hands of the Annes that offer me drinks
Our Annes that always promise to take us shopping with trees in
the car when my wife and I are both shut-up in the house & sick with
colds

August — September, 1970

Poem for Max Jacob

If only my character
were as simple as Max Jacob's !

   my skin wouldn't drag
politics with me wherever I go.

       O to be as unnoticed as he
hidden by his nose and billboard cravat !
I could eat a cherry tart
without Africa screaming in my veins

   I'd grow a beard
for "aesthetic purposes"
Although I hate aesthetics
   People would say "There goes SOTÈRE"
    Not   "Hey, there goes *that* guy—What *is* he ?
Middle Eastern   Or sumpin' ?"

          I wouldn't regard blondes
as evil
   I should pray more and look less at girls
   all the time
And keep my lists of the unshriven dead

Max have you ever forgiven unregenerate humanity?

I never have time to hang my hat
"I keep tellin' him he's my little Black boy"
      Brings me back to memories of 1964
   and   Dusty Springfield

I have sympathy with assassins

     That a poem to a favorite poet
should be so poor !
                  As when finally a man penetrates
The Woman of his dreams
with a penis twirling with frost on it —— lit
like a barber pole

   Indians invade the Supreme Court
        through my holey pockets

Thinking of you, Max, saves me from all disasters

    From the hourglass of
Tch tch sayers
Saves me from hot air
       from wondering

               whether
I am handsome And that there are men as handsome
or handsom*er* than me

   MAX,
    The shadow that they hunt everywhere is mine
  legendary double like "The Giaour"*
Although I am everywhere and nowhere

at the same time
(That was just a list of a *few* of the things!)

As the foot-pedalling of my friends whom I love
wins out against me the roads race ahead
You are the "Lighthouse of The Bride"

                                           June, 1968

* "The Giaour" is a poem by Lord Byron first published in 1813. *Giaour* is a word used by the Turks to describe all who are not Muslims, with especial reference to Christians.

I Am Outrunning the Years

I am outrunning the years
Night I do not know you any more
I knew one day I would be caught like this
The bullet —
hole sings:
The smile of a priest
Atop a brazen column
The ground below of white stones.

The girl who sells fried chicken at night
    in her cardboard house painted with red bricks
is very sad.
A turtle pulls the portrait of a fine lady
in white fur toward the smile
of the priest.
O labor
that is my mirror ! The eyes !
that incise the yule
of everyone's pardon

Everything is empty if one considers it empty.

YOU — now that I catch the ricochet
of the stars' Bakelite-fall——
"Manhattana" flies under your foot

The Dutch Catechism

for Philip Lamantia & Nancy Joyce Peters

Morning is always this series
Of broken half-recognizable tunes
That boys sing
While I'm outfitted in starched collar
And shirt
Living in a glass that blows bubbles
Not recognizing anyone
Whom I should know
It is like an orchestra of trees playing
With all their might
In an anonymous pilgrimage
Under girls' legs

Decalcomania
I am much greater than the snow
That has fallen
Only for a moment
In the absence
Of an Elephantine Principate

Some will say if nothing else
I had great words. Some will say if nothing else,
My friend, you had a great soul.
O that the two of these could
Have been combined ! But no,
I had great words but no soul.
Remember, my friend,
You laughed at the musical fish.
I fear I have the new identity.
The little man on the fire escape to heaven will be
Going into my eye.

I endure as many temptations as an eohippus
The birds eat my sorrows as crumbs
These are then made into
Pleasant songs
Of girls navigating their bicycles
Gliding into the warm wind

December — January, 1967/1968

Jeu de Noël Dream

for Giani & Carla Menarini

Ah ! Season of mellow mists   and shoplifters !
It's shoplifting time again and in the supermarket
The patriot with his baseball cap
Pulled down tight on his head follows me
Up and down every aisle !
So that I have to put the cheese and pastrami
Back   I'd like to give him a double shot-gun blast
In the head but he might turn
Into a Gorgon then.

I am the reindeer in the Tunnel of Love
Who watches his own TV Spectacular
A la Lapland maid and her lover
In their nuptial rites froth
My balls and with a smile
The sun and the moon do a dance before
She takes her **bi-i-G-G   CHOMP !**

She holds the sachet   up
Ecstatically in the air &   they dance

Meanwhile

I turn into a white carpet

From Lebanon

That rolls deep into the future

As California splits off from the U. S.

And falls into the sea

Anya

for Anya Wozniak

Your coming and going leaves a big umbrella over
The land Tomorrow where deaf and dumb mutes attend mass
The steam–roller whispers you its secrets
Trojan horse of exposed photographs !

How dark its hollowness like the hollowness of my heart
Which I know is extremely awkward But to whom *else*
Would I have told it and whom *else* would have so understood
With such dignity as that of pubescence gliding by on a bike

Like Berenice this book touched by your hands at the beach
At the moment when you discussed nudity I could see in your eyes
The clay pipes of the stars one by one being shot by your teacher Jacoman
I stand now in the morning dumbed like a bird

I track the spots you traveled Civil engineers going by
In their Ford trucks think I'm insane
But no matter for O the crushed tin plates of campsites
And your hidden places of feces !

Poem for Tom & Angelica Clark

                I fly on Spanish song
                O daughter of the great heart
                But I'm losing my job

The Rockefeller Building on the Moon
for Kathleen Brummal–Torregian

I am the exotic animal you've shot at the North Pole
From whom you've stolen the brown map of Caillers
                you're running along the telegraph wires
You can't run fast enough Telling your friends
You run down my age   the broken matchbooks are singing
an Alleluia chorus for you
       "When you make love, do you think of Hedy Lamarr
             Debra Paget or Maureen O'Hara?"
Ask the trains of Senufo masks. I tell them "None but my woman!"
I'm tracking like a hockey goalie   Another giant photograph like this
shot at the excavation of the Rockefeller Building on the moon.

In our quarter of earth a beach of gold lace is letting up
    sighs   The *Santo Niño de Atocha*
is dancing in his little top-hat
I've forgotten what I was going to say
But now I'm ready

    All the teepees have given me their fanfare of flowers

        In a kindly likeness the visage of Jean Metzinger
Speaking in undulant tones the constellations we've created

A large letter "S" caught in the Alphabet Soup in the periscope of the beloved

A House in California !

for Ted Berrigan and Alice Notley

Spanish night

Ah night of name-droppers !
Night of the decapitated plastic doll
How here in California it is like *The Night In the Gardens of Spain*
Our name is on the mailbox congenially in Arabic
   For those who speak of the jets of Eugene Ormandy
And Manuel de Falla !
I leave my piece of lettuce here on
The outdoor restaurant's patio table
        It will be found there in the morning

By   Sotère   Torregian.

After The Supremes "T.C.B." TV Special
for Anne Waldman

I mark the place of your poems with a dirty dead leaf
                and an old letter
Because I can find no other   This story can go on
                forever if I let it   So I stop
I pass the newspaper truck that bears the name
Of the famed "firm" where so many friends
Have come and gone

        A transparent Kiowa telephone-man who's really a counterfeit

Out of my imagination attacks me from behind   signalling
              A grey day.   Stopping to have coffee
Downtown induces this heavyweight squalor in me.

There is no paper   in my pockets

              Even to write my own name !   Pastiches
    cascade fall wigs
I am the only leper left with a muffler

So that a green stoplight   walking her child
Up the street does not even recognize me
Although now I'm myself
I'm reconstituted again !

I've lost my yen for crullers in the bakery window

   A slot machine
       looking like a rotting Shakespearean actor

December 9, 1968

For Franco Zeffirelli's "Romeo and Juliet"
to Olivia Hussey

AH, WOUND that breaks alone the sword   In art reprieved
      With the cries of passion of all the world
Lovers of all the ages as myself
I come to you simultaneously on a thousand walking feet
To all the capitals of the world, O you maligned
I come to you with my shallowness desiring to be filled

With the cloak of destiny my hands touching your shoulders
Lovers of all the ages I come to you
I name you my plethora my science of the last things
My Mecca of eternally trampled dimes
In my recaptured citadel self-confessional of the rose
All Africa comes to you

O Taj Mahal ! Your towers lull in their nadir now
But footstools for the wind *their* true breath is gone with Mumtaz
Your secret letter, Vauclause, opens daily its aureole
      Grotto of Petrarca and Laura   for the initiate
        of the firmament   textbooks of your desire

O Lovers of all the world
      simplicity of lattice and transparent insolubleness of
              porcelain

Lovers of all the world
I come to you
I place an invisible rose on your tomb   an infinite prelude
to my life   rose of the unknown

O Warsaw now with the ominous silence of vestal rain
Black Orpheus thrust forever into the mountains
Of Eurydice   Bahia   Hero and Leander   The Hellespont

Verona   unopened and unnameable silver
pearls beneath the grating on which I step   Your blood signed
        the contracts of peace   your boredom   our daggers

O You final martyrs
Carolers of the rings of Saturn   Aurora over the cities' sleep
Lovers of all the ages
I come to you
On the plain grey like my bowels where the word "Wolf" augurs
        a taboo   the word in all the languages of man

To my brother Othello Moor of Venice   and
To my sister Desdemona
                            throat of candelabras
On the Spanish Steps   /   Lovers of all the ages
I place an invisible rose on your tomb
yet an infinite prelude to my life

Apocryphal Poems

Awakening to the Eroticism of California

I.

O   SAMARKAND   !
Wafted in California by the theme music from James Bond's
    "You Only Live Twice"

In the Wonderful Year

            I wind in and out of girls'
    erogenous zones like a tunnel of love shell-shock their simpleton
    I come out unscathed but still beautiful
And they are unscathed & beautiful. We've been
Juggling mirrors   and won all the awards
Money comes flying at me greenback bills of flying fish
My so-called "enemies" forget my name through ice cream
Land barriers to Samarkand. Dream of the past.
        Hit by a car bled from the rectum but am miraculously
                cured.   It's great news
In the great year I am the only poet in America to win
A color TV set Should the "splash" I've picked match with
its contrapuntal "splish"

        which never existed

II.

Let me be fascinated as the eternal gaze
Of Zenobia that looks out across the desert curtain of Palmyra
That descends onto the night of our intoning
Lips

Where in the aisles of mirage before us the mendicants are wavering

We have finally arrived
Beached by a boat of your sister's
Which drums make artful gems
O Mistress of mistresses !
Captured by the salt taste on my tongue at the foot
Of my grandmother's statue of Zenobia the word I always thought meant
       " grain"

          Summer, 1968

"The Plough that Broke the Plains"
in memory of Frank O'Hara

Today I walk in and out of the doors of
    your death
With a farmer from Nebraska that fell from
a 75 foot tower
and became a maintenance man
He is my guide as Virgil was

Shining fire-extinguishers
sweeping the stairs

There are obvious epithets
A hatchet falling and nearly missing
a cartoon turkey
a guardian angel-type ghost admonishing a packer
not to stand under the elevated crates

The grandson of the plough that broke the plains enters
   blonde with a red ribbon on his chest

"O lover of wheat
Shall I get the big knife

I'm mostly anonymous

I don't know why the cooks are happy
they're almost dancing"

For Giuseppe Ungaretti

homage to Langston Hughes' "A Black Pierrot"

    I.

Because there is no music
You can see the miniature fire-hydrant in her eyes
About to squeak
Because of the lady lawyer with the sweaty palms
Who won't talk   Alas !
I walk over this earth never having learned her name

Over the floor of the earth that combs its blonde patched
    hair / speech taken away from the Nez Perce.

    II.

I feel like Machiavelli
Stealing these red gold green and blue ties !
Filling my order for everything
                           except the "gold"

III.

In "The Night Has a Thousand Eyes"
My partner in crime comes forward
    an old itinerant fountain
Who's useful for no one any more

Vendors' cries of the streets like the minarets
That I remember of my childhood
That I hear no more

                                    August, 1970

Cameo Piece

A bird in the hand is worth two poems in the uhh head

    The Poems need some food
Poems that Olwyn's Dream could blow !

        Poems far from the madding
    crowd   When I cry   Poems

          Shopping in the supermarket   Poems

    I'm the patient you're the doctor   Poems
Operating in the Poems   Early Poems late Poems
    What's tomorrow Friday Poems

The Poems are getting thinner and thin—
                ner.   No problem !

  Poems that create Enemies !

Come up and see me sometime Poems

                    Won't help Poems
         Believe me Poems. More Poems Excuse me Poems

Poems of "middle passage" What's for dinner Poems ?
            Sorry you didn't think that was very funny Poems
I can get along with the best of 'em Poems

            "Surprise ! I've rearranged the *entire house*" Poems
Ugh, tuberculosis Poems
Carmen Caballero Poems ?
              Everybody's getting into the act Poems !

   Help I'm drowning Poems
It's Alma Ata or Alma Mater Poems
You're coming I'm going Poems

Why *can't* I be the poet I want to be Poems ?

                            December, 1970

The Sex Life of Arshile Gorky

"Arshile—Vasdanigh!—My great star of the Armenians
still as I view the love-cry of your paintings I recognize
they are ever mixed with my blood!"

"I Thirst"

THERE ARE BLUEBIRDS on the breasts of the women of
        Armenia
I approach them as a wooden puppet
Made from the hanging trees of all nations
There are blue candles that are stuck in the sand

If the women speak the change in my pocket
        jingles
If I'm tone-deaf or tongue-tied I have no choice
But to kiss their nipples or to lick them off
With a handkerchief they've given me out
Of pure love

The Sex Life of Arshile Gorky

When the telephone rings and I can't get to it in time
It's Jeanne Moreau calling about
somebody's belated birthday party French library books
in a fireside chorus
enemies who will in the near Israelite future join the ranks
of the counter-revolution with their full force
stillborn babies of Hollywood in limbo drag priests by their
beards clinging to their altars in the sacrifice of the mass
up to you Arshile
the silver dollar with the million dollar legs dances at your
grave during a time when you have not yet died
It has a tendency to behave "very nicely"
When it doesn't know my tears are making rain
on the other side of the earth
"The news is out"
Please tell me what I can do
It is as if I were petting the sex of a flower
Where am I Earth pentecostal battleship?

If you could always see new wonders

With every American cannibal family

nature's revolving fans

& the trees with tires hanging from their branches

singing their eulogiums

magnified by the beautiful wound on a girl's

thigh   So am I

like earth on a winter's day

with every American cannibal family

having breakfast on top of me at 3.00 P.M. in the afternoon

Each with its bevy of vivacious children

so learned   I feel like

an ignoramus

in their presence

To Arshile Gorky

If you were alive today you would have been
  the victim of a traffic accident struck down unknown
Or convicted of murder a vagrant of the heart
in your long great coat because you could not
stand the girl whose voice ran even when silent like a
      chicken
with its head cut off to haunt you even in your dreams
Your shadow would have shunned you coming down
the walk even then
Connecticut would have never been placed on the map
You would have an early breakfast with the moon
on a deserted railroad tower
 Schoolboys would not have entered you into *their* notebooks

of masturbation
You would have choked on the brine from a wave
of the sun nowadays
The words in the secret mushroom would have never
been pressed in the hands of a blind girl
The song *Dead End Street* would have never been written

My Mexican girl friend seated beside the driver in a red
sports-car would have never saluted me
I would have never known her anyway
I would have never entered the tunnel as an ashough*
and exited as
the accordion with spectacles that passed me who would have never
said Hello as my shirt tails spat EPHETAH ! Be you opened to
the long rows of the 4.00 P. M. children's movie matinee
over in the gullet of a giant Trojan horse really
shaped in the form of a tin elephant of Uranus
For the modern musician the guitar would have never
    been
accepted as an instrument but for lovers there is
nothing but the guitar
But for the guitar
I would never have been born

---

*Ashough : "Enamoured" from the Arabic *ashegh*, a term applied to the
Armenian troubadours, who are said to date back to the 7th century.
To become an ashough is considered a high attainment.

Arshile Gorky—25 Years After

All
These loneliness's all these barriers all these
Spanish windows !
You know so well ! You know
The politics of the buttocks
Of the tennis-players just returned
From their game &
Drawing up their lace castles of what is impossible
To others
People eat before during and after sex in the
Same voice of the river bank

Ah,
All the stupid dimes wasted for   "Rides
  home" !
All the stupid looks wasted by others to show
That I, like John Keats, am a freak of nature
"You see" all the paternities of the world say
"These theengs have been spoiling my stomach"

You who are more golden as you give your eyes to me
As you pass I keep them for an eternity
That lasts as long
As the "exoticism" of me is rubbed away from your
    slate

Everyday of my life Arshile let me hang
this sign on my heart "Goodbye my Beloveds"
My Achilles heel the wound you misspelt
Everyday dogs of the Rich attack me I kick them
I shoot lightning from the Empire State Bldg. out
of my eyes & crash rocks   But it does no good.
      The night accumulates my tatters
There is not the freedom to walk where we want to
    anymore.
Pick-axes close the gates of tennis courts
Remember ! Remember O streetlights the death of Trotsky
        in Mexico !
My original sin & the sin of all locks !
Betrayed ! the Hare Krishna Jews dance
"Folk dances" on your grave !

"The Unattainable"

I hold the night skies in my
   hand
The night skies that are eternally
   Montclair !

Ah baskets of stars

I am blind

Stars of the body

Stars that are the beginning
and end of my departure

I contend with the world
like an elephant with his
Elephants Burial Ground
Snickers
make a castle where I enter

   Proud
   To fight a duel
   I can lose.

"The Liver is the Cock's Comb"

    It's raining red hot dollars
        The waxen head of a nun in the backseat of a car
        is teeter-tottering forward and back it seems with prunes
        for eyes
If I have to copulate with the Chosen amazon I meet on the street
        The Ploughshare's in convulsions
        because of the pottery of certain preadolescents
        it has entered its showcase out of good will
        I don't eat veal instead Fourth of July sparklers
        I'll see you on Monday
Because language isn't important
        A blade you stick in the window slit you get air that way

    for the purse of toucans with one hand if you wish

"The Black Monk," The Painting Gorky Was Working On The Last Hour Of His Life

Nor the comet that came unannounced, out of the north, flaring
in heaven...Then departed, dropt in the night, and was gone...
 – Walt Whitman, *Year of Meteors*, 1859-60

Snakes are eating other snakes.
They are making a long train out of the unknown of your name
The musket is putting on its coat of fleece.
To make the known unknown and the unknown known
Wisdom married to blindness my Brother that is my worth
"But the wars of the intestines" you ask
You have haunted me this long
I see the postcards of the great cities of the world and secretly

I see the tripods of lights long burning in the pyramids hiss softly

Arshile in the great masses of Africa silent for now
Only in your words unspoken
I am with my solitude tired mixing a tea of stars
While the adepts abound

O shepherds on the plains of Saba blow your reeds
      unknown in your rituals of baptism   To The Dawn
In the winds of the Empire State Building ! — Today
For this one column 2 inches by 5 inches in the news -
      paper of winter
Where the name of Arshile is mentioned in passing only
As a shadow is passed through by hordes of downtown workers
      at the noon hour /   and passing through them leaving them
                                           behind /
    There is no citadel for that fame where "the statue may bow"
Searching for a country which may never exist

Sharing the fullness of its silence
And like the dark side of the moon the silence of
    its fullness
Graven in the Marian crags of Sourp Khatcha
In the crater where the saint balanced a whole lake on his
    head   like a shimmering tray

Song For Woman

Song For Woman

— To Her Tomorrow Always —

*Woman is the Queen of Harmony, and that is why she must be at the head of
the regenerating movement of the future. Woman is higher on the scale
of Love than man, and when love comes to the fore, then Woman
will be the Queen of the Universe.*
—The Abbé Constant

WOMAN AS I KNOW YOU You are
ARIEL
Come from a thousand pogroms   of the world
I am the blood of your body
Where the sun hanged   Where Ivan The Terrible
Desecrated you in nightmares
Making the sputum of history your altar
        saying to the slaughtered
            "Here, there is no difference now
Between a dog and a Jew
For both
Are of the same religion"

WOMAN. When I am buried in snowdrifts
I think of this   I love you

Woman

When I see the nuns' dispassionate pity as they pass

In their flowing garments on the streets I love

YOU remembering that deflowering nuns

Was the Ukrainians' favorite sport

And mauling the beautiful Leah-lei

Was the Hungarians' favorite sport

Even feasting on her genitals

At the dinner-table

O WOMAN

When I'm lost in snowdrifts drunken I remember

       The whole world is a Woman !

At night I see neon lights are her eyes in their Dolores to me

And I do not care what the stalwarts say

That it is "neither here nor there"

      Woman when I'm alone an oasis blooms

      On the far side of where you're away from me always

Woman   Woman   scandalously I say
You have been my whole motivation !
And I have gone to search you
Out in the empty parks of autumn
Decorating myself not with leaves
But my life's bloodstained pages
  When Ivan crucified
You on his
World-center tree
O Christ-Woman
And I was born of your blood
The world's
Pogroms against you
And I desperate to find in what age or village
Your blood was flowing
I came to buy
The white-winged songs
Of other lands

    You were the enslaved *hetaerae*
    Under the mask of superstition
    And there your blood was flowing
    I came
    To mourn
    Your death
    And found my own a child of earth
    I came
    To find that you were WOMAN
        wandering forever in the world

Where you could see the upholstery of life's disorder
And landscape of
Man's tongue
On your heraldry of pain.
I have paid O Woman
I have paid for the sins of men against you

O in mulifoliate   passacaglias
Woman in your subject / object machine of laudanum
You take Quetzalcoatl as your protector

    Sun's sweat-box
          Among abridged queers
File drawer
For everyone's destiny
Except the
One you want
You want every one
Your destiny gone crazy
The one
Who wears
Her dress too short
Whose legs are those
Of Mayakovsky's Tatiana
Cosmic legs (she's pregnant)
And the one
With a birthmark
On her right leg

The one who faints almost
Going out the door
Of her own fragility

The ones
Who know somehow WHO you are
See your face sweating
Like the sight of Ingres' *The Turkish Bath*
Where the sun
Escapes its rivets
In the afternoon soliloquy
And gives you her eyes
As souvenirs

    From Iceland

And you can make a necklace out
Of them
To put around your hibiscus
Everyone's pregnant
Or looking for their other halves
Who've left for the rolling seas of N-a u-s i-c a-A
Everyone's Counterspy
The jig is up !
Against Machine-gun Woman
Machine-gun men

Everyone thinking you look "familiar"
A houri maiden from the Muslim Heaven flies away.

WOMAN

These are you phases

Through which everywhere men turn

I see them

Listen as through Orphic windows

The night blows in the scent of basil leaves

WOMAN they lead you a prisoner through turnstiles

Everywhere away from me

To a white-flower land where you're manacled
                                        always before me

Being led by your father

Being led by your lover

The summit I must go to, to sleep again

In order to wake and see you wither fountains

I light to you my eternal vigil

Of ignorance

Tomb of my unknown arson

   Heresy,   Avignon !

Avignon !

Knights crusading for the "true faith"
                                    wearing your insignia

Will slaughter me

I await them in the godless continuum

Of my nightmare

Men reduced to women, women reduced to men
The one gentle hand hacked off
And in the crucible merciless
The mutilated body of Woman
Learning from her childhood on to be a shrew
In a theatre
Where she will never speak her lines
And causality rots her bones: "The maiden's spinning song"

I shout from passages of the *Pervigilium Veneris*
But my head only lifts
Saluting the wind

Under the camouflage of autumn
My parable will be a hymn to you all over the earth !

  O Woman Unknown
Riding the expressways of retrograde dilemma !
Baudelaire's blind men following you on the Orient Express

To the disappearing cadavers in this Capital City
Of love's blasphemers

You have escaped from one slavery into another

And as I watch the proscenium
You pass
In droves skirts berate your "unknown malady"
You watch your doppelgangers
Punchy girls who prefer to joke with bawdy men at the shore
You prefer *these* dreamers, demigods
Who sing praises to Arpège's Aphrodité
Making their hadj's to the men's shops   downtown

His name is always "Frank"   On your lips
He will always haunt me like a Malay Archipelago of disaster
Like a monsoon
In all the returning seasons of my heresy

Under the flags that have rifled your birth
My eyes are goldfish
Your stop to read a monument

Whose words it has been granted me not to see
But the inquest is a gateway
To the lapse of your own bartered life

When the dismembered clock of the Empire State
Resurrects itself
In silver advertisement
Like the ball of the Old Year going out
Businessman will fly
Your genitals to their booty
Like a jolly roger

And across the street
A suicide rings his atonement
To you
Making your strained pelvis of *Triumph Stretch*
Almost plausible

Russian Woman, all for the cosmos you go with
    A rose in your hand

              Valia   ВАЛЕЯЙЯ !
You'll never see me
In Lenin's house

Your unabashed messiah undeserved Christmas
        they've sent you
My black horse
In the glue factory an unanswered oblation

The grail forever in exile
You're cautioned by traffic lights !
Vampires of unspeakable trust guard you

They strip the priest from his altar
                        In your sorrows
Your face looks exactly like your mother's !
Such indisposed warning !

You'll never know what happened "Womanchild"
Expose her nuptials obituaries

Watusi warriors string heads of famous lovers

      For you

And in the circle in which they dance
A diadem, a living dais for you, they are obliterated
Like a filmstrip of the night's entrails.

Grande Amoureuse – Anouk Aimée

    Grande Amoureuse,
I collect Anouk Aimée
All that flows in and out of her
The armadillo god emblazoned
For a moment in the carpet's lightning streak
In the Nile that flows in and out
Of the window of her neck awake
To the wind coming to me at 1.00 A.M. every night
All my life I collect Anouk Aimée
La Tête contre les murs *La Maison sous la mer*
Her being a boy in the newspaper of my adolescence
     Titles of her pictures sigh to me
    like baseball cards flared up
 And it is no longer "I" who am
Doing the collecting but me who is collected
Your eyes say:
"I like New York in June"

Then it is the birthday in your eyes of *The Metropolitan's*
  Assyrian sphinxes

   the newspaper streets split down the middle
STOP

In the morning
The little boy in the front seat of the car speeding
Through the underpass waving goodbye
Has no time to take with him my smile.
All preceding letters of the alphabet fore and aft
Stop before you
So that before air and water the name ANOUK
Appears in the naked sky airplanes and air
Bow before you
An orchestra of dates is crying in
Its sleep leaving me canonical as a sapphire

The dreams of your nights are the milk of the earth

Awaited one,   in this arcane,
Finally binding the hours home and brushing the lapels
Of the calendar with its sad monocle !

Your Gentleness to Quadrupeds   alights
*   through a vertical corridor*

A giant doll's leg drops through
With the sound of snow falling through a chimney
Down to the life-size fetish of a Dahomean prince
With diamond tiara who waits endlessly
In a carefree gait with future eyes

Anouk we ride together the only passengers on a train
Made completely of multicolored hedges

A music box sounds through the crash of a window
It plays *Plaisir d'Amour*
Laying down its cup untasted

As long as you're alive you carry me a thousand
Life-times in epitomé
On the silver tray which you hold
Of my likeness which all at once mirrors
Each image like the judgement of souls by Anubis
On the plain of titans our reposing red suns

For an Unknown Princess

for Donna Selvaggia Borromeo d'Adda

You sleep you give alms   of leaves you awaken
The trophy is destroyed that the wind has made
of the grace of your hair a few hours after you were   twelve
     years old
There is no partition between the sky and the dollar bill
              I hold up to the sky
Incendiary hands that close the lid of day
Each time you step forward you step back
The Atlantic plays its lullaby of salt and bones
A wedding is going on continually under the summer sky
I ride its entourage of children's clanging cars with sparks
     into fall
and afterward I am left stranded with my baggage

It is better on receipt of a cleaning ticket   that you meet
my struggling with ignorance
For your great ancestor Borromeo hung on the gallows
     of purity and laughter   There is no mystery

Now

The Poet and the gunman arrested in your reflection are one

Your Name of Gazelles
for Leila Khaled of Palestine

Leila   which   means   "night"   Leila
Who brought down the great whale threatening the world
Night, you have become my eyes
O salmon rushing upstream through Autumn's inverted post office
   In my childhood I thought the flies attacked me because
I had "colored blood"
For the very reason   that John Wayne won't forget the Alamo
     Death entered   in the registry of a bastard order
A language found to fulfill the need of the age
Displeasing to the profane as well as to idiots

As inside me the word "Spain!" melts a cathedral of wax
    into tears
Bandit Queen of the Sky ! When the infidel armies of myself
Had given me up for dead in the waiting room
  of Jewish dermatologist doctors Rosewater & Jacobs
In the day I had no memory or name but the routines of handshakes

And   pityriasis rosea   "a classical case"

As shells sound of the ocean
       & the sun blazes
With winds which rise up   and sweat which flows down
Ptolemy's map of the ancient world mongrels me
In its litany   Leila
With your bullet-shell for a wedding ring
In front of one you appear a frightening old man from Tierra del Fuego
In front of another you appear a young princess
With a sudden marvellous beauty

Your real name of gazelles floating like a slow motion film
      of dawn in Africa   on the wing
As I see the listlessness of the desert overhead flying
Where for nine months you have been the captain of a death command
        "No one will know where I will be tomorrow"
The moment is close for our returning "home"
Only when the vessel is totally drained is the last drop

Emptied out
"And that's how I came to hear my call of duty"

You are separate from the equinoctial wisdom of my life
Because of the severed hands of my flailing which you alone
    know
As they reach out to you
Haunting me so long now, in search
Of you   I'm a walking teepee delving in and out
Of libraries for your story that disappears
In the print of the magazine pages little by little
Week by week
As I come to grasp you more

The "Passionate Affinities"
for Madame Roseline Alric-Cleaver

"To you who prolongs my days"
I feel all my faculties taken up suddenly from their beds
As if they were prisoners lacerating the night with their silence
Of them taken away captive and shot
My discipline is lost
In fancy invitations desert bananas and tripod monkeys
As the days become more strident
      It scares me when I see the intensity of abandon with which
            the dance is rendered in our time
That cannot comprehend itself
Holidays come all at once and appear with cripples on walkies-talkies
      Outside our bed
Wolves of the new year yowl / O Woman of my Future
All naked except for the Apache dancer's mask you wear with its crest
      of the Four Directions

Movement is the key word

Sitting on a manhole of rock music that moves on an ocean of ice
That moves to sympathy frenzied then frozen in blue light
      broken by remembering

These days one pays the same price for a movie as for a book

Cozumel The Isle of Women where I work beneath the cheerful tingling
      of the rings of Saturn
With the same affection for young women who wear a neck-brace blonde in winter

The stewardesses cross a nation while you sleep
My metabolism !
All sane people are now changing time-zones flying overhead
You're causing the compass needles to go mad
As I drink my toast of rum to all of New York
Like the Wolfman on a night of the full moon or a Yezidi outside the walls
      of Babylon !

The clouds play their organs and motorcycles
The Indians return their $24.00 for the Isle of Manhattan !
People look at you as if you were a crazed killer because you've signed
Your rent check with the wrong date

The cameras come in slowly on horses' hooves
Into the church of my sorrows of the blood

Take their picture (flash) there in the shadow

How can I get to know you well enough when each time
You are a different person a house in America is robbed
It's as if you had never remembered who I was when you find me again

The dizzying silver fan of bottomless burlesque spreads
Its opiate bridge across the ages

It's best to familiarize one's self with the scents that remain
               In the absence of love
And the particular way the innards react
      When the words Caf-fe LAH-tayye are pronounced
It means that I have this intimate feeling for you
That in some way you should be as untouched as the beach
        that tires in an ebb   the more I talk
The less I know what I am

O For Words when I am unable to write in the night !

The woman of myth the woman of reality painted by Delacroix emerges
        as Liberty   storming the barricades
In you a thousand women speak in tongues of the lost
      language   I turn only to the sperm I hold in my hand
Young woman too shy to speak to me on the avenues of the day
The "Passionate Affinities" of Nefertiti and Marie Curie are within you !
So also the day books of Marco Polo that behold the radiance of
       our bodies' embrace on the plain of the invisible
It has been said you were born of
                     my rib and yet I know it is not so
   It has taken me all my life to find *that* out until now

That Spanish galleons laden with treasures have emerged from
        Your desire by which all the earth lives !
             the spirit and lives of poets in your smile
Each age   in your absence all the earth comes
To know you again   as Persephone   in the advent of winter
        who watches her pursuers   and rescuers
The now awesome astronauts who thrust forward in a vestal gallop
        to the music of "Shape of Things to Come"
                in the exploration of mountains on the lunar surface
Waving their arms wildly in their moon-car yelling "Yahoo"
        like cowboys in reeling intoxication

In the quest of the unknown you REMAIN   Radha and Primavera still

The one Dante spoke of as "coming before" you bathe with your many maidens
In the golden river even in the eyes of the women from Kentucky
I fill myself with music and there is your smile the many shy gazelles
        of you playing in the evening garden each leaf I take is the note of
                a guitar
The notes all vanish at your footsteps today Memory the flowers blown past
The kiosk of my life   Dusk in Paris   Morning in Delhi

On This Day of Confluences:
The Unpublished Preface for *The Age of Gold (1976)*

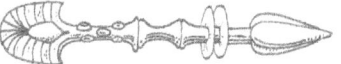

> *Prenez ma main je conduirai loin*
> —Paul Éluard, *Vivre*
> ("Take my hand, I will be leading afar")

> *Tu es sur la rive adverse hirondelle*
> —L. S. Senghor, *Par de la eros*
> ("Thou art on the opposing shore swallow")

On This Day of Confluences a flame burns from New Guinea in the Pacific and its art of totems to the splendid masks of the Dogon in Mali to the Paleolithic cave paintings in southwestern France: that flame, which burned brightly with the painters of the Lascaux Caves, resides with us still. Therein the Poet still has his or her *mission* or, as my friend Senghor argues in his writings, his or her *vocation*. Vocation coming from the Latin *voco vocare*, or calling, in a time when these conceptions seem unfashionable, or even unacceptable, to the surrounding society in an age dominated by the sciences of biology and technology, —thus, to create, to unify, syn-thesis, —to give the primacy to Love, to Liberty and the fulfillment of desire—this primary Eros that moves from darkness into light, that perceives the Dark Side of the Moon and the Light Side to be as one and the same—which is the bridge of the Conscious and Unconscious minds: it is this which is the vision of Poetry.

The poetic moves not with the head alone—as you students are wont to conceive through the tyranny of English classes and their incessant intellection—but, as the ancient Troubadours of *langue d'oc* used to say, with the heart, with the motive force of the whole faculties, mind/heart, soul and body.

If we are to analyze, let us say, for the moment, the strange writings in the Book of the Apocalypse for its rational meaning, we would find that none of its poetry makes "sense." Analysis was not its original purpose but syn-thesis, to plumb the depths—which the French *le poésie* knows—where poetry is always at the heart of the Marvellous—*le Merveilleux* of the French surrealists.

Techniques of the psychic life reach to a ladder of the Unknown. In the Arapahoe Indian Peyote Cult, as is documented by the eminent Classicist C. M. Bowra in his groundbreaking book—introduced to me by my friend the poet Joe Ceravolo*—*Primitive Song*, a poetry is chanted whose meaning the initiates themselves do not understand nor can comprehend, that is, even in the Arapahoe language itself the words don't make sense or, when translated, the words are rendered into non-sense sounds. This poetry, in a sense, invents its own words as it goes along, much as Tristan Tzara did in the early days of Dada or as Joe Ceravolo did in his epic poem *Fits of Dawn* in the early 1960s.**

Thus I contest it is this same atmosphere that pervades both the mad visions of John of Patmos, the visionary poet of the Apocalypse of the Christian Bible, and that of the Arapahoe poetry, a mysterious terrain, in which one discovers revelations through the Marvellous. As I understand it, it is this discovery which Shelley spoke of in his *Defense of Poetry*; it is what the Surrealists brought forth with their automatiques and experimentation of poetry; it is what so-called "Primitive" men know about the nature of poetry, which is *Illumination*. These same frenzied "Illuminations" with which Arthur Rimbaud changed—or challenged—the consciousness of generations to come. Attitudes conveyed to the English-speaking world by poet and mystic William Blake at the advent of the

---

*Joseph Ceravolo (1934-1988) whose *Collected Poems* (Wesleyan University Press) were published in 2013.

***The Collected Poems of Philip Lamantia* (University of California Press, 2013) has three examples of sound poems: "Scat," "Babbel" and "New Babbel," circa 1955-1964.

Industrial Age in England and, later in France, by Mallarmé and in the Twentieth Century by Apollinaire and the French surrealists, and in England by the surrealist poet David Gascoyne—to whom I am ever indebted in my own becoming in America, along with André Breton's exile during WWII and his subsequent residence in New York, thus becoming one of the lineal godfathers of the "New York School" of poets and artists.

It is in this meeting of the Conscious and Unconscious minds, Dream and Reality—so-called (or waking) where the real forces of poetry lie; that is true for African society as well as in its modern contemporary adherents of *Négritude*—and again to whom I am ever indebted in my own recognition of my ancestry—who bridge continents, I speak here, particularly of Aimé Césaire and Léopold Sédar Senghor, both of whom associated with the French surrealists, and it is true for American Indian poetry as well. It is a feat of Love, this love connecting all things which is the motive force of Poetry; Love which gives us and takes away the worlds and words we cannot speak with one "fell swoop" the binding logicality, which before has seemed so commonplace. This is where the *You* in the sentence across the page, the *Tu*, the "You, the reader" are just as important, just as essential to this love if you but open to it, leaving behind the task-masters of the English classes, as the Poet has so opened himself or herself as an *Open Sesame* in the process to create a new consciousness.

I say then I remain a prisoner of every foreign language that is not the universal language of human desire.

"This path has freely chosen me. The idea of 'success' or failure is at the end of my foot..."—Jean Schuster and André Breton, *L'Art Poétique.*

"Those who enjoy my poems should say them when they are alone and their doors are open in the night. Those who enjoy my poems and who love have no longer any need of them." *Ibid.*

IT MUST BE NOW, MORE THAN EVER BEFORE (whatever 'BEFORE' was).

It remains: Poetry is the force of liberation, soul and body. Liberation of all men and women from fascism and its undercurrents. To enter an epoch where we live the challenge of the poetic as much as the poet does, in the direction of the Marvellous, and thus eventually realize the challenge of total human liberty !

Once again: VIVE L'ADVENTURISME !

Address originally presented at
Naranja and Granada Houses,
Stanford, California, 1970
for Betsy and Claire

Redux Annex

"Diego Rivera's Rocketship" – Janina Torregian, 1974

After Mayakovsky

for Anne Waldman and Lewis Warsh

The aureole
comes into my room
and says
"Wall Street"
I say
"Hi!"
My eyes generally qualify for topaz
The farts! They ride in big cars
and see me drop my last piece of tuna
to the ants
I stuff my magic letters down the
throat of the cyclone
The aureole crosses its legs
  like it has to go to the bathroom

Now we spar
smear street kisses
Dutch.
On my day off
I have lost the continuity
but I shall not forget the aureole.
This may be our last meeting
before the Big Ticket-Taker.

Like chicks in the window of lechery
keep a diary

In our afternoon
shoes without socks
that wind clocks
and cause anger.

My definition of "patriotic"
is: to lead all the chandeliers
of the world to one watering
hole.

My hair stands out
like Brussels sprouts
in the night
when I tell time
by our sun dial.

In disastrous
situations
girls
always are seated
fixing their shoe-straps
on a corner
and I
— a fire-plug
keeping my
desolate banner
in my pocket
ready to unfurl

I've just kicked over
my "interior castle"
its nipple
and gear splatter
into the street
A dog follows me
  stupid and somnambulant
like the lion of
St. Mark.

When I take
a break
I smell the sea from
this hospice window
And I stride in labor
the library sea

above those cabbage heads
and gramophone horses
where below
the wind sings
to the girl:
"I'm asking
I'm asking"

It was the birthday of a king.
Oranges.
That I, a snow drop,
cordoned

The aureole !
the aureole won't
give me a ride anymore
The aureole's put me in a closet
 where I can't think anymore
but of the Hopi
word for "snow"
today
my neck
is a siren
calling firemen
to the ice palace

When I reach out
I am always the song
that someone has
forgotten

I like anyone who defies
the Cops !
The birds talk The new school that is starting
loyal tastes
The aureole !
I want to tell her
how difficult it is
for me
to be a poet

But barriers punch
I laugh
like a stone statue
astride myself
flapping
in a black homeland

Summer, 1967

(Farewell to) The Newark Library Reading Room
for Calvin Forbes

I have a new home. A roaring Sparring Partner like a
    sunspot
Orifice for the grey membrane theodicy & lexicon of my
    laughing years.
It is the Public Library Of The Skull
Where everyday round the clock poor old vagabond-eccentrics
and alcoholics enter.
The vagabonds jest with the librarians; tell them their jokes
    lives and troubles
O Harlequinade

And the librarians grow hysterical up their left sleeves
Until I can see a zigzag shape grinning and I know
These winos are the real harlequins !
An old waif in breadline clothes and tattered hat reads at a table
Back issues of *Better Homes & Gardens*
And from a strange periodical called *Gourmet* he righteously
    scribbles down
On frighteningly vast tracts of scrap paper and paper bags
As if the world depended on it.
I must get away from these harlequins.

It is in this smudged lapidarium that I look for my Chanterelle

You are between the resemblance and the divine image
It is my blood that flows down uncharted streets of
Dreams where in the monotone cleft
You are motionless between the resemblance and the divine
      image unreconciled
There remaining I find the eternal scansion with which
      Eratosthenes
Measured the earth and the lips of the heavens

1967

I Discover Jean Valjean Everywhere

We see these pearls   walking in the morning   They do not know
         who they are
but we know
the true conquerors jasper landscape
One "Beastie" after another
Papa
Shifting sands
Bottles and
Suns and Earth

I am proud of my zero
The boxcars rushing through me in succession
I am Jean Valjean
A challenge to any interior
when my loves say "Garbanzo"

You harbour a hag but it is beautiful that you do
It is what makes your name stand out
It is what makes you beautiful
This pristine brilliance
O Camino a Los Cerros!

I take my stride

My legs are giant totem poles

that cause a whirlwind wherever I go   wherever I have been

O feathers of Youth!

I will not leave you orphans

I will come to you again and again

O gyrating feathers of Youth!

May 24 — June 7, 1967

Vers Les Printemps

" Tout en marchant Jean jette un coup d'oeil sur le étalages "

"Very There merchant Jean has a quick look at shop windows

poeme-objet :

S.T., 9. ix. AD2008

poème-objet
S.T.

Rosa Alchemica

homage à Ann Sheridan

> *Mais chante sur mon absence tes yeux de*
> *brise alizés, et que l'Absente soit presénce.*
> —Léopold Sédar Senghor, *Élégie des Alizés*
> ("Yet your eyes of tradewind breezes sang
>   upon my absence,
> And that of the Absent Woman's presence.")

You are skiing
You are holding the dummy's hand
You are skiing again
Aired in furs you enter the great hall standing in
    the doorway
You pose in a two-piece bathing-suit
Showing off your buttocks in a back-pose
Again on the skiing trail
A young novice bows before you her eyes flash electric
You appear again on the divan a siren
You are at home in front of a *circa* 1940's fake fire-place
    relaxing in shorts
You emerge like a Clytemnestra
With serpents spinning a sunburst on your breast

1967

The Open Car Door of a Dream

The open car door of
a dream
three days of agony
when your telephone rings
Like the messenger nails doing the soft-shoe
shuffle of Golgotha.
When I step outside
the giant's heavy breathing starts
at a breastplate beside my door.

The room growls,
My listlessness hackneyed
all day of newspapers

O night that I slept in the window
of African drummers
O orchid where I journeyed
in the No-Man's Land of
calling out
for you, in the green of the
number 4,
imprint which you left
of your going.

1967

On the Birthday of Pablo Picasso

Today I ate a baked donut

I saw the woman who rebuked me in love

She was having breakfast with a hairy-man
    (One of the Boogey Woogies in Laurel & Hardy's *Babes in Toyland*)
Hoo ! Boogey Woogie !

There is nothing like a beautiful morning
When you don't care about the woman who has rebuked you
              in love
The fountains open up a pathway
Happy birthday Pablo
I walk over the path the fountains have made for me

Everything is imprinted with this sadness of non-concern
All day I have been driven completely mad
By an imaginary hair on the nose
I would sound this clarion to you
Everything is imprinted with this sadness of non-concern
And I am not concerned with my non-concern
Although I wish I were somewhere else at this time
It is as if I were standing speaking with the gift of tongues
On top of a Lapland hound

                                          October 25, 1967

Crossing: San Andreas Fault, April 1968
for Martin Luther King Jr., (1929-1968), in memoriam

Et ma voix s'ouvre dans le vide
– L.S. Senghor, *Élégie pour Martin Luther King*
("And my voice opens on the road")

Yesterday cocoons whistled down from the trees
Like conga drums
Whose hands were silenced in sand.

                        In a portico reminiscent of the Alhambra
            I walked   wishing to be forgotten   only for a
moment

In the hot sun   in the cold fountain

With a slit down the side of the skirt

Assassinating lutes

            . . . .

Today, at San Andréas Fault

The bullet
That killed Martin Luther King
O world on wheels   has pierced me   through

As the Fault pierces   the countryside   as the power-towers
        pierce the sky

The mute Braille alphabet of the Ocean shifts.

                        April, 1968

L' Adou, The Woman-Enemy

for Linda Slotnick

I nibble on cookies in my office

And my brain is chased by an immaculate
    pillar with an automatic

Her hair the colour of the desert in its fierceness

To meet John Hawkes in Rhode Island

The French jewels of Amal Falluti
O Adou !
My enemy

I saw taking refuge in a sandwich your double
                          When I discover
                                        her
She says, "That's all right. Everyone takes me for someone else these days"
through mouse-glasses

I want to cry for her
But I continue on my way

The many times I've passed unknowing

How soon your Cantabrigian house has stopped
singing
Every time I've passed it like the Egyptian Army in the Sinai
of 1966

In that way I meet you
You and your amazons who cry
      in their *manœuvres* bayoneting mirrors

                                  1969

On the Eve of the Moon Landing
July 20, 1969, for Kathleen

Day by day, London is sinking like a hissing diamond by the weight of its
own tears. This while Bonnie, a youthful monkey blasted off from Cape
Kennedy a week ago, pushing buttons and receiving food pellets for her
efforts, slipped slowly into orbit

Dogs with mysterious passports come in the middle of the night
and chase you around cars
I'm not Flash Gordon I'm Buck Rogers
We must beware of imitating ourselves. The Red Star Linen service
across the street sings a cradle song
by nature the cold hands of July as well as January

Martyrology of Spring on its translucent-paned doors

Thousands of GIs of the 1940s using the word "frig" for the first time in
the "Theatre of War" causing a new wave from the *Lunar Mare
Pamphilium*

The gardenias in your hair and the cactus in my fingers when they touch
Maskers pass the Cape Verdé Islands   in search of

The prize, entitled The Mouth of Truth   with my mouth

An old Black beggar with a turban approaches you and tears
off a piece of blank white paper and says:
"*This* is your future."

I wave Goodbye with my poor hand-less arm the mule and the sawmills
The cloistered nuns in the deserts of Arabia send you
a blackmail letter but we destroy it, counteracting their influence
A fascinating mission To challenge you to find a sharper blade than
   myself   To be naked in the middle of a thunderstorm in the middle
of a forest in midday We assassinate the TV Weather Girl
who explodes into a — *Sqwaak* !

Just as men land on the Moon
When a lady sits on a horse, it's one thing, *but* when
a horse sits on a lady, well, isn't it cause for cutting flowers and leaves off
Lilies of the Nile — and sawing down and carting away a tulip tree?

Anyone so inclined to play the game
had better stick to the adolescent kissing brand of "Post Office".
A massive lock jamming is soon to be underway !
How is it we are always going separate ways
When always we are together,
      moving toward each other !

                                                    July 18—20, 1969

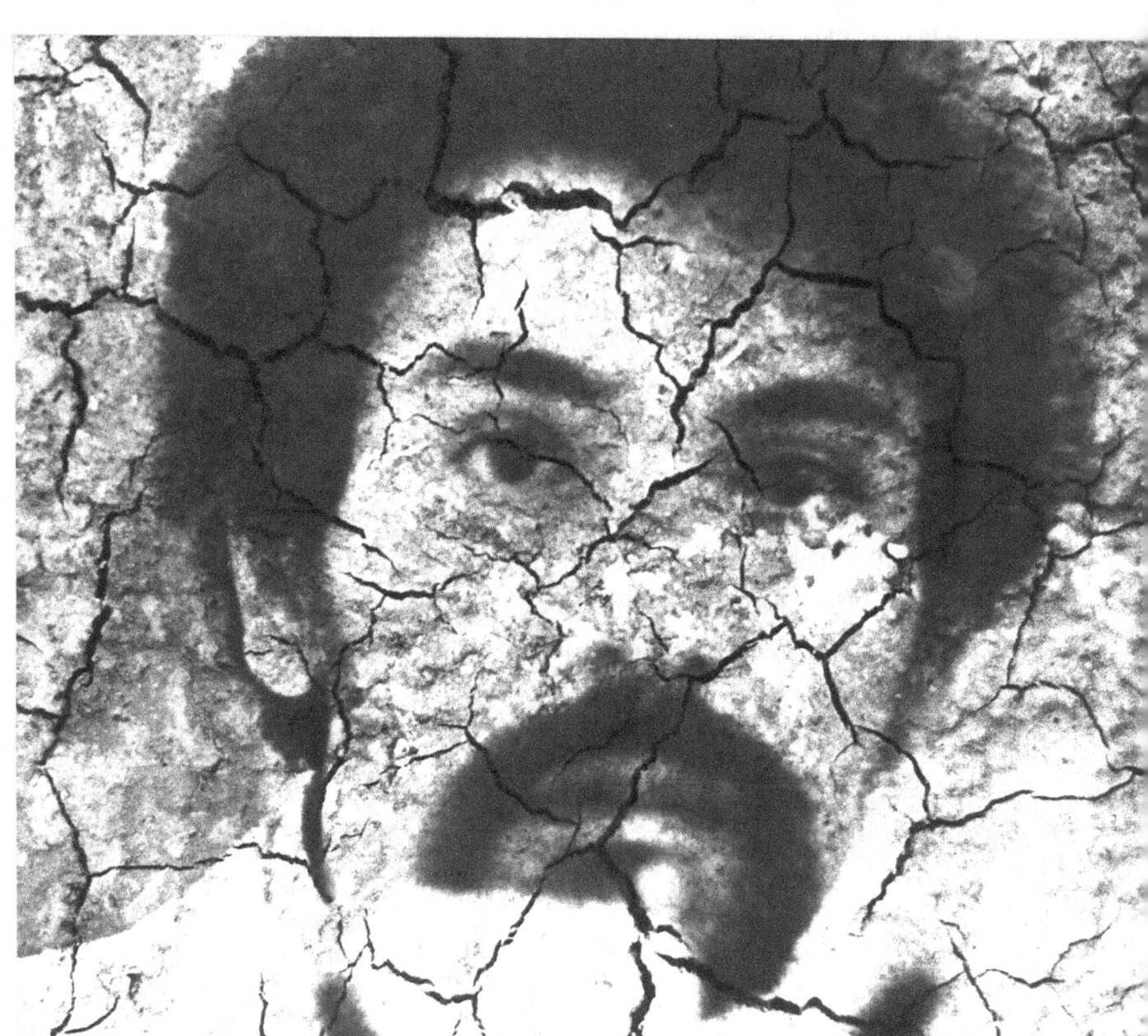

Forgetfulness

(in Arabic)

I.

Your eyes are two Parthian moons that weep
over the lilt of the desert dune at dusk

II.

Desolate
I stop beneath the ruined arch
   of a forgotten bridge
where there lies an abandoned bottle of wine
A sunburst jogger like a flame comes dashing by
     calling my name

"Night People" in San Francisco on Sunday
for Philip Lamantia and Nancy J. Peters & Maureen and Mike Smith

Like Alaskans a whole troop of them roaming across the street
With their white-fur mufflers and Antarctics of ermine
Emigrants of the New Ice Age we do not recognize

On the curb-stones an orchestra of Aces-of-Spades
                                       playing music
    like one of my daughter's first learning to say "Goodbye"
    through windows

A knife beats in my breast
The tow away zones of black snows

I enter the *Tosca*
Italians at the bar call me "Africano /
                            —*Siciliano*"
We all have to get up by 5 A.M.,
which never really happens anyway

The emigrations go on flying their saint balloons as we pass them
GHIRADELLI SQUARE   with its neon–necklaces
                                     of shoes I am never sure
Which really comes first
Night "the tears of a mother" the people
Sunday or San Francisco?

Forget it all completely Come back again

Like taking rancid cosmetics out of a secret closet
and giving them to your closest friend for a present
                                        or speedy breakfast
What are the rose cobblestones praying?
While all the denizens are carrying Polaroid pictures in their pockets
of "sleeping late"

Just as sure as the word "work" should never be mentioned hereafter

In the morning my friends say they see me pictured
       on a *Moulin Rouge* type poster everywhere
          like a dirigible of milk
                the wind of the sea flows through the
          lattice of my waning
  memory

A russet wall plaque of the goat Aries with a white stomache is
the eye of San Francisco that never sleeps

                                                January, 1970

Point du Sable

for Kathleen Brummel–Torregian

> *une monde d'exploite d'aventures d'amours*
> *violente*
> —L. S. Senghor, *Nocturnes*
> ("a world of exploits of adventures of violent
> loves")

The martyrs of Love
Are disfigured
As they pass by swooning
coin disappearing money
The martyrs of love leave

Forgetting their proper names
The martyrs of Love
are incorrigible
fly into a panic
of horses over the headlong traffic in the future

By sewing back the days
of sleepless nights
Into an orbit of palatable selenium
With the thud of babies
Falling like weightless interplanetary rocks
Giving no birth-date
Oil of palms in the night of Time
Alchemical water which seeks to become fire
was not meant to be at all

The martyrs of Love inhabit the rooftop houses
of pigeons
in search of a new star
Their long voyage always begins from
an indeterminate starting point
The martyrs of Love
are centuries-old tortoises/solitaires
in their shells
Their lips become a road wounded by its thrust

Palo Alto, 1970

N. B. : *Point du sable* can be translated from the French as "speck of sand". Jean Bapiste Point du Sable (before 1750-1818), known as "the founder of Chicago", was a fur-trader, most likely of Haitian ancestry, who settled on the mouth of the Chicago River circa the 1780s.

On Meeting My Friend, Mengistu Lemma, in San Francisco 1970

for Mengistu Lemma, (1924-88), Ethiopian playwright and poet

The waitress is still
saying: "Is everything okay?"
They're ripping the lines out of my poems
& putting them on others' books displayed
in shops   Poems by children are doing
better than my own
The Way to Become the Sensuous Woman by "J"
will appreciate my work

I meet a man who says: "I dropped my razor down the sink;
I've never done that before."
And then proceeds to call up on a phone a plumber
named "Sugarman"
I tell him I'm waiting for my wife   "That's something
to wait for," he says

South San Francisco is wearing its mitre and regarding me
from a distance with its own "language of stone"
with its savage breath of commuters
The beautiful female mannequins in the show-windows
attired like men in fashionable outfits of fringed suede
and autumn hats like cowboys
are chasing after me as they exit out their windows
with their jeweled rifles   lovingly
a little arâq will defeat them

July 24, 1970

Oedipus Complex, Here I Come

Oedipus Complex Here I come Oedipus Complex Oedipus Complex here I come Oedipus Complex here I come Oedipus Complex here I come Oedipus Complex here I come Oedipus Complex here I come Oedipus Complex here I come Oedipus Complex here I come Oedipus Complex here I come Oedipus Complex here I come Oedipus Complex here I come Oedipus Complex here I come

OEDIPUS COMPLEX HERE I COME OEDIPUS

Here I come Oedipus Complex here I

Oedipus Complex here I come Oedipus Complex

in collaboration with my two daughters,
Janaina & Tatyana, Palo Alto, 1970

"Duck Soup"
with Mengistu Lemma in San Francisco

I'm not in good form today

The devil cut the rope and the saint plummeted 1000 feet
Then flew off with six wings on his back.
Ah, Duck Soup!
In a miniskirt I ate with a poem in Ge'ez for *sauce*
Confucius say: HAVE DRUNK INSIDE
                (Bad for Health)
I—I'm in love With you O fire escapes
—Round and round we go
"O Brown-Skinned Girl" don't wait for me; I go
                              to City of Hankow
    The Angel—arrested for flying over Times Square
with Barbarella (Jane Fonda) in his arms shooting peas
from a pea shooter at "hard hats" and businessmen below
I'm asking

                The City, dressed as a beggar, who am I?
Plastic pants are now creeping out the door of the bar,
    but there's no escape
Except through the gate
of green-headed dragons and fish

Playing street signs as guitars to the moon I can't see

——"But! I was in Houston and saw it there"

Ah ha, there's the fire escape! Where's it go to?

To the top of the moon ! Dear Passerby
    I find myself at a loss
for words, I mean, I think I'll drink some more beer
Is everything O. K. ? Yes, but not with the science
of sexology. She always comes back in that miniskirt
and well cultivated smile. *Mais oui !*

Makes me feel like a second-story man that the State of Israel
aims to shoot down (Missed again, guys!)
My Armenian-sounding Friend
                                    Who
can't change his spots so to speak. Tell me,
am I not now transported
to Harrar drinking beer and wine with *Rimbaud himself?*
Quick call for the Ark ! (rather encumbered
    on the heights of Mt. Ararat between Turks and KGBs)
              There are many
Tasty Middle Eastern delicacies here in the City
Also in Cairo—just don't ask there for *matzohs !*

Yes the smiles of beautiful women   always vanish
when I receive them
I'll sing along with
Robert Redford and Paul Newman
"Raindrops keep a-fallin' on my head"
You should open your umbrella, then but choose not to !

                                                 1970

N. B.: Poet Mengistu Lemma, friend of the poet, disappeared in Ethiopia in 1976 during the dictatorship reigning at that time. Ironically, the dictator's name was also Mengistu !

"Come Back Africa"
for John W. Franklin
— and In Mem. St. Clair Drake (1911-1990) —

        The peacock does its dance with shovels
           COME BACK AFRICA !
   The long procession goes
   with the lights of its helmets down

Into a Dantean hell.   There's no Francesa
   nor cool of hail.

The letter signed in murder

laughs when it sees itself in the mirror.
What will I do with my soup?

On the contrary there's magic in whatever a Black Man
touches
the railway the masses the drums of the *Metro*
Satan's chimneys unloading everyday their dromedaries
     in seraglio —
pajamas who step in leaps and bounds

These are

more than *just*

moteefs to be dealt with in the film and "integrated" into a poem:

   a. children's tin band playing
   b. Makeba.
   c. wife's murder (?)
   d. hero's enemy

¡Xotho is the language of hell where one must always
refill the bottles of hooch stolen from
the closets with water
that will not kiss you unless you give it five dollars

Unless you first spit
before you enter the door
Zululand of my soul you come to meet your Father
Dance playing the white goats as sousaphones

1970

Che Guevera

I find there is anachronism within me
A Third Law of Thermodynamics of a shrinking sun
Which guards itself
from the Pacific's sentinel-eyes
There are those who are commissioned to keep the Status Quo
on Earth (thus is the burden of the poor insured)
It's true my natural inclination is to prefer to be as much
as possible in the company of beautiful and lively women
Like the character of the eighteenth-century aristocrat the *Scarlet Pimpernel*
My shadow's always tested against the Cave

Of the coffee house ! Like the Wandering Jew with hearth burning

   inside him   with radio turned on full blast in his head
to ease him of his anonymity
and the world's misery

Yet forever Comrade I am a man like yourself with no home

I can never be at home in "this world" or in another
Its music divides my body from my soul

I search after each young woman who can be found
with her book open to the unfurled picture of
   . . . .

The concertina squeaks out from the depths of the Bolivian jungle

In a bit of asthmatic smoke   it says "I know how my life can be justified"

    Why, Comrade, you lived and died   and here is
a generation blinded by
its own *hum*, moving, rising, upward
like a helicopter I within it like a scrambled egg
it carries away both myself and the Mona Lisa's smile
   (along with some other doubtful artifacts of the age)
coming toward you CHE with a need
for direction.
So we see these signs in the Gothic monuments in the public

   lavatories effaced with graffiti. A moon park dark
and part bright side   which is where the entourage
of the voiceless move toward you
Where they *become*
One with a voice in the image of your
              death at Villegrandé (*perfume of
Michelle Rey's Parisian bell-bottoms in
the night*) vision of a rainy windshield   your eyes
drenched in formaldehyde

Thus the slow dark caravan moves across Asia Africa and the Americas

When I walk in the night and look into
lighted cellars I see old unredeemed legs looking like ham bones
sing with wizened voices: *"Hambone Hambone where ya bin"*
calling at me as I rest seated in a wayside hothouse nearby

A giant beanstalk sprouting upward hatched from
a classic torso centerpiece
I watch it spring into the air
as I sit there breathless

    With my album of old loves and those that are to be
    I'm weighing lighter and lighter
    The Nightwatchman comes with jangling keys
    to lock all the doors
    I rouse myself from my *cauchemar* *
"Preventing the Death of the Cities" I carry a Christmas tree
As the last really "great"
                            Comedian of the Silent Screen . . .

But here with CHE I find my destiny
O Refugees !
O you who sleigh in your sorrows on automatic weapons !
Palestinians Men and Women of the *ANC Mozambiquiens*

You are now my homeland

   wherever you are
                roaming
You take my language and my race
and whatever I have known of beauty.

                                        1970

* *cauchemar, Fr.*, nightmare

For Groucho Marx

No poet ever won the Irish Sweepstakes
Because a poet's fate is to weep at the stake
In Monte Cassino the stones are laughing
But on the road I travel they weep
Like poor little poets without a muse
The discovery of cannabis is attributed to the Chinese
Emperor Shen Nung about 2700 B.C.
And to Emperor Asoka of India who founded the secret
                                  society of the Nine
Unknown Men— he knew also the horror of war

O series of photographs showing the shadows of the moon
That makes the jade empress cry
I will dry my tears and fade into the
        Sea of Tranquility
The Boxing match in the snow !

The ice on the lake cracks
As I skate backwards into a frozen moon
The chapeau of the egg
More brilliant in December
But it is the aura of the life inside
That crowns the egg

And when it cracks the shell
It takes its luminous shadow
With it.

Knock knock   Ah, the long-nosed poet !
Laughing Buddha
You teach me so well to cut a hole in my shadow & walk away

From love
A poet cannot walk away.   He must play
        (For she is always there in every laughing stone, in
            every piece of jade, in every egg, and moon, love's
            in your shadow too.)
My book will remain open to the eternal mystery
Of the eggplant !
And love will reveal the mysteries

You still do the world's poetic work

                                        Sotére & Kathleen Torregian
                                        1971

The Ghost of the City of New York Appears in California, May 25, 1971

It's all in a day's work   the doors from Life to Death

Muhammad Ali comes in one door and Russ Meyer comes in
   t'uther   While Ali
      Stages a CONFAB at 11.00 AM but doesn't
show all the cameras and tape-recorders are left

With their tongues hanging out in the heat
Under the veranda I just recover from food-poisoning & look up

AUSTRALIA AND NEW ZEALAND SHAKE HANDS
How'd you *doo*
It is prophetic I meet a child born at the same hour
and day as my oldest child
I learn   your Anglo grandfather became the
      Arch-Archimandrite
Of Alexandria "for all the Greeks downunder"

MOHAMMED ALI GIVES his speech finally "On the
Intoxications OF
LIFE" (That's for *Real,* Folks) and tells one girl
sitting up near the stage to
pull her dress down because it was "showing"
above her knee That's *it,* it's all Over wham boom!

Now Russ MEYER must be the "greatest" genius of America (?)
His "genius" lies   in that he is the only one to successfully
make blood spurt from a victim
on the silver screen like a slide trombone carrying a hilarious note

                     .... So
many things have happened The People's Liberation Army
has seized the Israeli Ambassador ('Ray.') Bedford-
Stuyvesant exploded again (I wonder what's happening
on Killens' block?) and lava has overflowed on (Mt) Aetna
       (again)
 Can't keep up with it alll
This Hermaphrodite   running up and down the stairs with
a sword   Hey!
The doors slam open   the crowds emerge
Like an age ashamed of itself
Like an elephant with a cauliflower ear   Some are doing

       a St. Vitus dance and shooting fireworks
out of cactus-launchers

You come toward me like a diffident haystack
I'm talking to you all the time you pretend not to hear me
You're with your two pals   (One of them the "returned" of
       the Boogey Woogies) the road parts us   like a part in the
       hair
of the whole Earth   and splits me with it
The stars make a sound like a tuning-folk
Maybe I'm learning anew language to speak a new language
       Maybe

What is this   Cult of the Fedora hat
and the jalopy of the heart ?
Rose of Lima   Unbeliever that I am   I believe in you so much

"Plebiscite"   "Dolores"
. . . .

"Quitting Time"
Washerwomen in the elephant grass *'re* listening

Once again I come upon an evening 5,000 mi. away from
        (New York)
the mirage of "The City" become so obsessive
    I see Skyscrapers appear moving through the fog
on horses' legs !
    "With no interjection..., *oh?*"
New York my poems are always an elegy to *you*
The horses see me coming
the horses smell the sunset wing   *Zapata* ... in whiteshadow
still rides on it
    Golf-club-headed exorcized Jewish demons
happily hopping backwards

                                    May 25, 1971
                                    2405 Alpine Road, Ca.

The End of the Era of the End

for Robert and Bobbie Creeley

"For once I'm going to try my hand at writing poetry"

Once a year we all get together
In faraway places   like Bolinas   or
Vesuvius and sit around a table.
It looks like a board meeting of some gangster
organization but if you looked at us you'd
know different. We expect to see the little
electric trains going around the table serving everybody
sugar in their "tender" cars
but it's not like that at all really
      By the time we all get together, our group
infinitely expands   People can't deal with us
We really need telephone lines set from one end
of the table to the other to talk to each other
                    Someone's forgotten to bring the
    tape-recorder   (Bill Berkson)
when we get together it's the end of an era
Or the era of the end I'm not sure what

We remember all of our respective names
Although in some cases it's been years
since we've seen each other
the Era comes in on its high horse the horse
is drunk   we give the horse cups and cups
of black coffee but it doesn't help
"We're fucked"

A stewardess from Irish International Airlines
comes down to earth and serves us
drinks   innumerable drinks
"The Green Death"   (*Rainier Ale*)
I find my name is *on* "The Enemies List"
with some of the most dangerous *revolutionaires*
of the country   an exciting development !
"On The Mesa"   A new anthology of Bolinas writing
Our escarpment says   "Recent Visitors"
Which is free to all   Something's wrong with me
I'm never the same after these meetings
Summer begins   the great silence between

Wife and mother   All predictable
You should drink plenty of orange juice after you 've
been drunk all night   Remember it has a sobering
effect   Andrei and I plan Vampire castles in Transylvania
   Let's pretend we're a great sea and Tugboat Annie
is coming over us   But the Era gets jealous
We're not paying too much attention to it anymore
The Era starts a fight with Joe Brainard (I can't keep
up with who's winning) The Era is a *bully*
I'm sorry if that doesn't sound too American   It's the
only way I can speak

Tomorrow the end of an era begins   I have to go
to work   "Church Windows" by Respighi
When Bobbie Creeley was a disc jockey in Albuquerque
I was a child inside the heart

of a pilot   with memories of Arturo
Toscanini conducting the NBC Symphony Orchestra
of the air Meetings are so sad the music gets lonely in the
background   We're back to our little game of hide-
and-go-seek again   After you've gone through all the sexual
positions you've got "*Ha-tha* Yoga". Ha-tha Yoga says
"Hi there!" I haven't been crammed in four years with
so much "literature"   as I have been this week
Vesuvius is beginning to erupt from under us
It's clearing it's voice   in the demonstrative way
   a bartender does when he wants to be *paid*

Bobbie Creeley begins the first lines of a Collaboration Poem
          It goes "Oh!"

It moves from one end of the table to the other
It's out there somewhere my pen's been passed around
with it   the poem's taken on so many new contributants
                                    it's uncontrollable
It's gone completely out the door

                                        June, 1971

"Lost steps of the goddess in the land of the Morlocks (by way of the Time Machine)."
Poéme-objet, by Sotére Torregian

The Longest Day of the Year

for Ausma Jaunzeme, Poet of Latvia

> *Entre l'ennui et la manie de vivre*
> – Paul Éluard, *Le Travail du poète*
> ("Between the boredom and the mania
>   to live")

I am looking for my love's country
What have you done with it?
(*See Blue Card Inscriptions*)

I've kept the image of the Star of the 17th Arcana
  of the Tarôt
in my pocket all day as a possible substitute
for the Miraculous Medal

But the sun never takes a good picture of me
In its files I never recognize myself
as I think I am, but it is really me after all
I knew there was something important about today
besides the fact roses dip their feet in the hour
It's not Shakespeare's Birthday

But that's pretty commonplace
A boy choir plays golf
in my "Babylonian Captivity"
This is the day
when madmen with rucksacks on their backs turn around
and go forward in search of the post office of the infinite

I Did Not Know It Was
the Shortest Day of the Year

I did not know it was the shortest day of the year

That is, until you called me up and told me
I looked in the Daïnas *
for clues
they said it was the shortest day of the year and
the shortest night on earth for my people

I hear desperate calls from the Far North

What have they done to my Ligo * fires?
I listen but I don't hear   They have taken away
destroyed my Ligo night ecstasy
    taken away the magic
pawned it for unreasonable reason
No, don't be too sure
it turns into a forest   Egypt supports Latvia
    lovers searching for fern blossoms
        Biologists refute

I put on my blue cornflower wreath

You do not walk with a rucksack   in the Taïga*
ordinary weeds become sacred
Tonight my people sing
No tears no sorrow no hunger no thirst
All wounds heal

Sotère Torregian & Ausma Jaunzeme

Palo Alto, 1972

* Daïnas : ancient oracular verses of the Letts; Ligo : spectral phenomena found in Latvian folklore; Taïga : prairie tundra.

The Mountains of the Moon
for Eiréni Alexandróu

> *Tu es la porte de beauté, la porte radieuse de
> grâce... ...J'ai promené ma quête inquiète*
> – L. S. Senghor, *Nocturnes*
> ("You are the portal of beauty, the radiant portal
> of grace... ...I have followed my inquiet quest")

(This beauty has named me, and I have lost my name)

The Mountains of the Moon.   Each night when I sleep, minute
caravans   come from the Mountains of the Moon.

First the *Sassanids*, then the *Abbasids* and *Almoravids*,
and then the chorus of the *Azerbaidzani* slaves,
where you are singing but I cannot grasp you.
You are singing like the little girls dressed in white,
whom I watched pass beneath my window when I was ill as a child;
they were the attendants receiving donations —
offerings pended to the sash of the saint being carried in its cart
by the faithful during the holiday procession . . .
I cannot reach where you are. I cannot have you.
I call out to you but my call vanishes in the din.

When I was that child, I saw the richness of your olive skin
contrasted against the white of your dress, socks and shoes.
I vested myself in a veil in imitation of you;
I wore it in order to *become* you, but that didn't work.
I wondered in my life when I would wake up to this music.
It has sat laughing under my eyelids all the while
when I have closed my eyes !

The *Sassanids* bring me weapons but they turn into giant
cucumbers. The stars of the strange motion
cannot even comprehend what is happening. The Dynasties,
in their sadness, come to me and shrivel into nothing
— all their obelisks, all their courts, all their satins !
There is only your singing left. It is they who have become
the slaves, my teachers, my doorman, my lanovacs.*
They are goats and donkeys now before my eyes arrayed
in livery. I feel so sad when I pass and salute them ...

The Mountains of the Moon fold up their umbrellas and
go home — backwards, that is, always without me,
poor taxis of *éboulement*, without their fare,
going into day.

c. 1972

* "Lanovacs," see meaning provided at the bottom of page 65.
N. B. : *éboulement, Fr.*, a crumbling away, cave in, landslide.

At San Juan Bautista, a Thousand Years of the Persian Empire on TV

for Maria of El Teatro Campesino, wherever she is . . .

Ah, you caught me unawares on my island of doubt

These kind of meetings are the things

That created the Wyoming Desert, perhaps

And when the silences of the adobe of the Pueblos
your smile as you appear
before me stalwart yet yielding   to abolish
            all the bullets of the *Rualés* in 1911
the kind of scream that stays with you from the plume
of Quetzlcoatl's temple long after you've left Mexico
hiding still in the morning mailboxes
in your eyes   Where on the screen I watch the long caravans
of the 16th-century satrapies on American TV
in a parade of a thousand years of the Persian Empire
on their splendid mounts all in their lustre before Queen Farah
(*These are the last days of the Shah and his reign*)
In the letter I've received it asks where's the "fracture
of my irony and beginning of my agony"

    (*The Great Gate at Kiev*)   How is it
Mussorgsky's "Pictures at an Exhibition"
Always seems to play
              on the radio on my birthday
My lithe saltimbique   *My filly-mime*

Headlines in the newspapers on the day of my birth June 25, 1941
("Europe is a disaster area")

Everything I do is supreme, that is, when I can
be indifferent to it all

As Lorca in the tradewinds

But it's now for *our* one moment in *l'histoire* as I kiss
you *Agitprop Danceuse*
from Oaxaca
Openings of space blossom with your
grace wherever I go !

                                      1973

In the Poor House of the Wind

for the Marriage of Tarun Bedi and Paola Barbieri

> *Plus léger et limpide est l'enfant que j'étais*
> Paul Eluard, *Poésie ininterrompue*
> (" More delicate and limpid is the child I was")

In the Poor House of the Wind
the Parthenon stands in Napoleonic rags
festooned with plumes
    stands at attention
The Bacchantes in their ultra-high frequency voices
serenade
on the edge of the mountain
of "dead languages" of Africa Central Asia and the Near East
And the Black Jazzman   in a "jam-session" with tears in their eyes
whale-oil of the St. Louis Blues offer you leis
so many leis
sweet Bird of Paradise   In the Poor House of the Wind

I don't know what is   shadow of moonlight gold
barnacles that surround me
long forgotten in the Poor House of the Wind
You come All at once in your flourish
As you proclaim "18th of August !"
I lose my credentials   in the vanished pearl smoke rising

Cantors of stained-glass trees
In the Poor House of the Wind
the chariot of Apollo Belvedere pulls up riderless
within it are two boots filled with the first words I learned
                "as a child"

Ticker-tape streaming of those words
flies over the avés of Seasons for the orator of brass
Arthur Cravan his lit cigar in his mouth as he declaims from his poésies
lost on that fallow shore of crickets
where Francesca da Rimini laid down her book
        fallen *quel giorno più non vi leggemmo avanti* *

After the festivities evening hits the pavement hard

I struggle with the music on my phonograph
As the beautiful crevice of sleep encroaches
to find me negligent

"repairer of the breach"

In the Poor House of the Wind where we dwell
Love as our good fortune

                                            Menlo Park—Palo Alto
                                            August 18, 1975

* "That day we read no further"

On the Anniversary of the Birth of Surrealism
25 June, 1917 — 25 June, 1974
for Mme. Hélène Laroche Davis

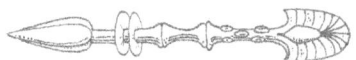

Chère Amie IT SEEMS THE ONLY RAISON D'ETRE that we should appear here is for Change. That is the only reason why the word "Surrealism" should remain in the wind and not be effaced. Complete and unutterable change from within and without. Change of the in-utterable. Consciousness and change (*plus ça change!*) of the existing social conditions which have plagued Man-and-Womankind from the beginning. Otherwise regard me as one before you as undistinguished from a flying sarcophagus in the air with the digitals of Paganini; regard me as no different than an epitaph for the tome of Love.

Regard me then no differently as you would an nonentity SHOULD YOU NOT PERCEIVE POETRY AND LOVE ARE ONE AND THE SAME ORACLE OF ORACLES AND THAT WE ARE COLLECTIVELY THE SECRET OF ITS DELPHI FOREVER. If there is not enough of atoms falling over the end of the world so agreeably provided by Newton, that it is not a problem. We will construct our own waterfall of world's end, and right here where we stand, beginning by *signing away our recaptured lives in a lover's kiss*, then writing a last letter in our blood that we will live forever. And that is the reality of Poetry.

In that reality all languages are borders of countries that are immediately effaced.

On one side of the calendar hanging on the wall, it is snowing, and on the other side is the heat of the searing sun in summer. And in the midst of these is Memory. The day the moment began remaining the same, the years began changing rapidly. And on that effacing road "The Beloved," painted by Dante Gabriel Rossetti, leaves and returns a thousand times each time with a new face and we are always wondering who She is... Yet *She*—ELLE—informs us first her name is *Primavera*, then (Nerval's) *Aurélia*, then *Isadora*, then perhaps *Nadja*, then (in my life) *Anya* Wozniak, *Roseline* Alric-Cleaver and *Helga* Liebisch, then in battle with *Simone* Weil (with the International Brigades in Spain, circa 1937) and comes again to birth as *Larissa* (LARA). The night passes. On the hinterland of the blue desert great stars come rolling and moaning with love-moans, flowing glowing in their light, ever forward beckoning then going beyond us to the meridian.

—Valorisation of our lives in the Revolution of Love and Poetry. Final victory and each of us its lone observer for no other reason—and what other reason is there for the darkness of the sky than to show us so brilliantly the silver with which the hoof of Raymond Lull's horse strode so elegantly into the church where the love he sought after prayed at the altar—an Unknown Woman !

And even so, what good is the darkness of the mind but to betray in like manner one of those aureoles of Desire ?— Desire kept in the mind and light kept in the society of men. But that light is a false light, not the light of dreams nor the light of a life lived in the *Other (L'Autre)*. That light which shines as Marcuse shows in *One-Dimensional Man* is not the light of a Communal Presence. It is the *light shed from the co-axial cable of the River Lethe*...

Years before and years after I am writing this, I write this on my so-called birthday, the 25th of June, date of the invention of the word *surréalisme* by the martyr of Love, the Poet Guillaume Apollinaire at the premier of his poem-play *Les Mamelles de Tirésias*. On that summer night in Paris it is met with nothing but hatred by the good citizens of that metropolis embellished in their own primordial ignorance. —It is always to this time of its first invention that I harken back rather than to the formalized codes *surréalisme* received by later interpreters—albeit my admiration for André Breton and his manifestoes of Surrealism. The year 1917 slowly removed itself from the company of men and

On the Anniversary of the Birth of Surrealism
25 June, 1917 — 25 June, 1974
for Mme. Hélène Laroche Davis

Chère Amie IT SEEMS THE ONLY RAISON D'ETRE that we should appear here is for Change. That is the only reason why the word "Surrealism" should remain in the wind and not be effaced. Complete and unutterable change from within and without. Change of the in-utterable. Consciousness and change (*plus ça change!*) of the existing social conditions which have plagued Man-and-Womankind from the beginning. Otherwise regard me as one before you as undistinguished from a flying sarcophagus in the air with the digitals of Paganini; regard me as no different than an epitaph for the tome of Love.

Regard me then no differently as you would an nonentity SHOULD YOU NOT PERCEIVE POETRY AND LOVE ARE ONE AND THE SAME ORACLE OF ORACLES AND THAT WE ARE COLLECTIVELY THE SECRET OF ITS DELPHI FOREVER. If there is not enough of atoms falling over the end of the world so agreeably provided by Newton, that it is not a problem. We will construct our own waterfall of world's end, and right here where we stand, beginning by *signing away our recaptured lives in a lover's kiss*, then writing a last letter in our blood that we will live forever. And that is the reality of Poetry.

In that reality all languages are borders of countries that are immediately effaced.

On one side of the calendar hanging on the wall, it is snowing, and on the other side is the heat of the searing sun in summer. And in the midst of these is Memory. The day the moment began remaining the same, the years began changing rapidly. And on that effacing road "The Beloved," painted by Dante Gabriel Rossetti, leaves and returns a thousand times each time with a new face and we are always wondering who She is... Yet *She*— ELLE — informs us first her name is *Primavera*, then (Nerval's) *Aurélia*, then *Isadora*, then perhaps *Nadja*, then (in my life) *Anya* Wozniak, *Roseline* Alric-Cleaver and *Helga* Liebisch, then in battle with *Simone* Weil (with the International Brigades in Spain, circa 1937) and comes again to birth as *Larissa* (LARA). The night passes. On the hinterland of the blue desert great stars come rolling and moaning with love-moans, flowing glowing in their light, ever forward beckoning then going beyond us to the meridian.

— Valorisation of our lives in the Revolution of Love and Poetry. Final victory and each of us its lone observer for no other reason — and what other reason is there for the darkness of the sky than to show us so brilliantly the silver with which the hoof of Raymond Lull's horse strode so elegantly into the church where the love he sought after prayed at the altar — an Unknown Woman !

And even so, what good is the darkness of the mind but to betray in like manner one of those aureoles of Desire ? — Desire kept in the mind and light kept in the society of men. But that light is a false light, not the light of dreams nor the light of a life lived in the *Other (L'Autre)*. That light which shines as Marcuse shows in *One-Dimensional Man* is not the light of a Communal Presence. It is the *light shed from the co-axial cable of the River Lethe...*

Years before and years after I am writing this, I write this on my so-called birthday, the 25th of June, date of the invention of the word *surréalisme* by the martyr of Love, the Poet Guillaume Apollinaire at the premier of his poem-play *Les Mamelles de Tirésias*. On that summer night in Paris it is met with nothing but hatred by the good citizens of that metropolis embellished in their own primordial ignorance. — It is always to this time of its first invention that I harken back rather than to the formalized codes *surréalisme* received by later interpreters — albeit my admiration for André Breton and his manifestoes of Surrealism. The year 1917 slowly removed itself from the company of men and went out into the night. It hasn't been found since. Only at one point was a beggar found "blind as Homer" seated in the street before a Barber Pole around the corner, holding out before him the certificate of the death of one Guillaume Apollinaire, dated November 9th, 1918. No one ever seems to put coins in the poor beggar's cup.

And those men who go into the Barber Shop for their haircuts there in the Aurora Borealis have never heard of the name of the first Surrealist, Guillaume Apollinaire... As a child I entered that same Barber Shop to be shorn of my locks (similar to those who dwell on the Ethiopian highlands) with that waiting presence outside seated there, undefinable — more than thirty years ago. I hadn't then heard of the name of Apollinaire either... But one day when all the women on the bed of love became equal with their partners, and a man growing in desire on the bed of love alone knew the name of Apollinaire—the aeons rolled past them, and a Stranger suddenly emerged with the secret of youth from those beggar's clothes: It was André Breton.

The year 1918—irrevocably over for all time...

And the year 1941, withal its upheavals and holocausts offered to the god of war, ushered in my birth in the world: and the wordless strangeness of finding myself a poet without being aware of what was then being visited upon me... the words...

—*the words* would only come later in my tenth year or so. I emerged from the Barber Shop of Aurora Borealis finding haircuts were no longer given there.

In time the *chevelure** of all those who had entered there grew savagely to the length of the Steppes of Central Asia, where all the dreams of Man-and-Womankind coruscated as black gold. As a child I was frightened by those dreams. But the year after my 17th birthday began my second birth with Surrealism. In effect I was born of Surrealism! This was a momentous discovery for me and words came begging to be my servants—but free servants—as I walked on the avenue of Broad Street in New Jersey with the aura of André Breton walking

---

* *chevelure*, *Fr.*, "A head of hair"

beside me on *La rue sans but* in Paris, France ! Proclaiming that I, too, was a Poet and my hands were slaves of the Western Wind—wind of Walt Whitman's *Song of Myself*, of Francesca da Rimini,—the Absolute of Hegel,—the Cumulus Nimbus of Karl Marx, and the revolutionary vision of Dorothy Day.

I tell you that out of the dissimulating blindness of this beggar *I saw for the first time*. It was the vision of *the Marvellous* !

It was thus your beauty came to me.

That is why those who take upon themselves the mantle of *Le Surréal* take on an especial interest for me: as I, too, wish them sight—collective sight as in the structure of the butterfly's eye. Justice then in this new sight will be opened in freedom; when Justice has stripped herself of her robes and it is we who have clothed her and all the opening and closing doors of all hours of the night whose lights mean endless bread and wine to feed all the peoples of the Earth. Those who heed me in this time will often ask how... how is it possible for me to actually believe these things ?

BUT I SAY IT IS NOW, MORE THAN EVER BEFORE, BECAUSE—

Nous Sommes—BECAUSE... *WE LIVE !*

And perhaps in ages hence this *Surréalité* will assume new names of Love and Hope, but as the police of Reason seek to apprehend us with our stolen fortunes, we will go aloft on the beautiful comet's-tail of Mohammed's horse—into an infinitely blossoming bouquet...

At that moment Hope will be travelling along in a dug-out canoe in search of land. And at that moment land will be sighted in a nameless country.

Summer, 1974

www.ingramcontent.com/pod-product-compliance
Lightning Source LLC
Chambersburg PA
CBHW080541170426
43195CB00016B/2633